Theology and Issues of Life and Death

Theology and Issues of Life and Death

John Heywood Thomas

CASCADE *Books* · Eugene, Oregon

THEOLOGY AND ISSUES OF LIFE AND DEATH

Cascade Books
An Imprint of Wipf and Stock Publishers
199 W. 8th Ave., Suite 3
Eugene, OR 97401

www.wipfandstock.com

ISBN 13: 978-1-49821-552-7

Cataloguing-in-Publication Data

Thomas, J. Heywood (John Heywood), 1926–.

   Theology and issues of life and death / John Heywood Thomas.

   xx + 136 p. ; 23 cm. Includes bibliographical references.

   ISBN 13: 978-1-49821-552-7

   1. Attitude to death—Christianity. 2. Future life—Christianity. 3. Unborn children. 4. Life cycle, Human—Religious aspects—Christianity. I. Title.

BT903 T56 2013

Manufactured in the U.S.A.

Contents

Foreword

It is an honour to be able to say a few words of introduction to this collection of papers from John Heywood Thomas, on behalf of those who have already known him as minister, teacher, and friend, and of those who are reading his work for the first time. Readers will find here a learned mind at work on a set of questions that arise in our reflections upon birth, death, and the future of the world, as well as a pastoral heart seeking to discern in the midst of these perplexities how human beings may be guided to their proper home in God. Such questions seem to have a particular urgency in our time, which makes this collection as a whole so fitting. Not only have there been unprecedented advances in technologies across a range of fields giving rise to possibilities for the manipulation and prolongation of life far beyond anything previously imagined. But these have been accompanied by a proper anxiety concerning human responsibility and freedom of choice that haunts moral debates and heightens the tensions between differing and often opposing points of view. Moral decisions in such matters as abortion, assisted suicide, stem cell therapy, and anthropogenic climate change, to name only a few, seem now to have become hardened into ethical stances, even ideologies, that are not conducive to genuine enquiry or thoughtful responsiveness to complex dilemmas. In consequence, society is diminished. An effort to speak calmly and intelligently about these and similar issues is all the more to be welcomed for its encouragement of individual reflection and political discussion alike.

The guiding conviction of this collection is that the work of theologians has a uniquely significant role to play in developing moral awareness and in shaping informed public debate on these issues. This is a conviction that cannot be taken for granted in the current situation, and we owe a debt of gratitude to Heywood Thomas for presenting a most persuasive and thought-provoking case for it. He does this, not so much by staking out a claim for territory or for some high ground above the fray. Rather his writing is an example of how moral thinking is carried out in the light of faith. It is an example worth following closely. His papers illustrate how reflection upon issues of life and death is essentially a search for human self-understanding—one that is difficult, because we ourselves are at stake in what we are trying to understand, and necessary, because in this undertaking that which most belongs to human being is exercised and so made real. For we become more fully who we are in the very act of thinking about who we are, just as we are directed towards the meaning of our lives in deliberating on this question itself and letting ourselves be led by what is learned there. Philosophy and theology are partners in these exercises of thoughtfulness. Their joint efforts disclose how human being is itself at risk in these pressing and stubborn questions of life and death. And they show how a deepening moral awareness brings the human being to its own fulfilment at the very limits of experience where we are stood before the divine.

The collaboration of these disciplines of thinking is but the beginning, however, of an open and generous invitation, extended at various points in these papers, to all scholarly disciplines to bring to a common table the findings of their research and to ponder together their implications. This kind of dialogue, this thinking through together with others, is a way of reciprocal enrichment and of active engagement in what forms society as a whole. While such conversations have in the past been entrusted to the academy (though this also may no longer be glibly assumed), the extent of their ramifications is far-reaching, touching immediately on the next generation of those who will in their turn play a leading role in their own societies, and spreading out more widely into the prevailing ethos by which social and political affairs are continually being shaped. Here too, Heywood Thomas conveys how theology that is grasped by God's self-revelation may hold open a way for humanity to be led into its most complete realization and final end in God's own life. Being essentially a pointer to this end and a guide to those who would find it, theology takes on a two-fold responsibility in public debate. It searches for the deep underlying assumptions that have brought about our contemporary understanding of human being and the world in which we are placed, bringing these into the penetrating but gracious light of God's word. Then it runs out ahead to discern where this is going, to discover that to which this self-understanding is directed, and to hear from that future God's promise to us of finding true life in Him. So it is not accidental that the final word of Heywood Thomas's text here is that great prophetic proclamation—all things will be made new.

There are many other good things to commend in this collection—its frequent references to poetry and works of art, its attention to the writings of numerous philosophers and theologians who have wrestled in their own time with these issues, its continued reflections upon the contributions to theology of Paul Tillich and Søren Kierkegaard, and not least its expressive style, which will fondly remind those who have been Heywood Thomas's students of his measured and searching manner of teaching. In a time when theology is having to demonstrate the value it adds to the academy and to argue for its constructive impact on the wider society, these papers are both resistance and promise of higher things. For in the end, Heywood Thomas shows his readers how theology turns these demands back against their sources, against the ruthless commodification of knowledge and the predominance of the age of technology that sustains it, so that these may be broken open to their own presuppositions and be granted the possibility of taking another direction. Questions of life and death and the future of the world are among the most poignant and crucial ones of our day, for we know ourselves implicitly to be at risk within them. Yet these papers are written in hope that we may not give up thinking altogether, that we may not completely forget to wonder about such ultimate questions and to search out their meaning, and further, that we have already been met in our own endeavors of understanding by a loving God in whom finally we are saved.

Susan Frank Parsons

Preface

This book began life with the series of three lectures which the University of Wales, Bangor, asked me to deliver several years ago. Though pressed at the time to publish them I was reluctant to do so and they have lain awaiting an appropriate time and context. Even then the theme of the book was an abiding concern of my career: since then it has, if anything, gained more importance and relevance as the various advances of medicine and the changes in society and politics have made the theme a matter of greater urgency. To put the theme in theological context and to amplify the discussion it seemed sensible to support those lectures with various writings, mostly unpublished. Chapter 5 appears in its original form but is expanded and likewise chapter 6 is a revised version of a chapter in Jupp (ed.), *Interpreting Death*. This final product has been made possible by the various kindnesses which I am delighted to acknowledge.

The skilful assistance of my good friend, The Rev. Blake Hemmings, must be the first which I recognize; for once more he has transformed my typescript into publishable form. I am grateful to Cascade Books for accepting the proposal, and generous and expert guidance of Dr. Robin Parry as editor has been invaluable. I give special thanks to Dr. Susan Frank Parsons who has been not only encouraging in the production of the book but also helpful in the business of publication. Well-known for her work in the field of Christian ethics she has been generous enough to contribute the Foreword to the book—a culmination of assistance greatly appreciated. Finally, I should like to mention the kind permission granted for quotation: Prof. Gwyn Thomas has very readily agreed to my quotation from his poetry and J. M. Dent have permitted the quotation from Dylan Thomas' works.

Introduction

When one has spent a long time, as indeed I have spent the best part of my life, practising a craft it is difficult to recall how it all began and what motivated it. My father was a blacksmith. His was an ancient craft both in Wales and elsewhere, revered as one of life's foundation skills. He had no difficulty in recalling what had first inspired him to wield a hammer and to shape the black iron into the useful forms of a horseshoe, a ploughshare, and the like. It had been his family's tradition and he was proud to take up his part in continuing that noble line. However, his own history was very much that of the twentieth century as he left the idyllic rural scene of horses and farms to become part of the emerging world of the motor-car, plying his trade in the context of the early spare-wheel which will give South Wales a significant mention in its history. So it was that, as semi-urban and semi-rural children, more akin to our rural surroundings than the town only a few miles distant, I and my family grew up inheriting not so much traditional crafts but a traditional spiritual culture in which craft had a central place. As the blacksmith's shop had been a forum of enquiry and debate so it was that the chapel was as much a source of intellectual enlightenment as it was a means of spiritual development. It boasted a "library"—a mere cabinet of books, the provenance of which I never discovered; but it was for me, a youth who had not yet progressed from the children's section of the town's public library to the adult world upstairs in the grand building known locally as "The Athenaeum," the entrée to the world of spiritual thinking. There in the chapel's library I first clapped eyes on those two spiritual classics, Jeremy Taylor's *Holy Living* and *Holy Dying*—to give them their proper titles, *The Rule and Exercise of Holy Living* (1650) and *The Rule and Exercise of Holy Dying* (1651). It is fitting to recall that these were in fact written when Taylor lived in South Wales, in Golden Grove where he was chaplain to Lord Carbery. I say that it is fitting to recall this because I am most emphatically of the opinion that Wales has never admitted her ecumenical debt in spirituality despite the fact occasionally that debt obtrudes in our hymnology. However, it is the lesson rather than the debt to which I would now call attention; for it seems to me that the greatness of these noble works is that their very beauty reminded us by their very titles even that death, like life, is a *task*.

Together with the chapel it is to my grammar school that I am indebted for the motivation to undertake a task for which that intellectual and moral formation proved so great an inspiration. Sometimes it is assumed that unless a school gives very obvious recognition of spiritual values it is interested in neither upholding nor cultivating them. This was not the case with my school because its recognition of Christian background in the Morning Assembly was as real as it was conventional; but it was no more prominent than its profoundly Christian ethos of consistent toleration and wide ecumenicity. It is in particular to my education in the Classics and to my study of French Romantic poetry that I regard myself as especially indebted. True, the works of Shakespeare, Milton, and the novelists and poets of the nineteenth and twentieth centuries broadened my mind. However, it was the encounter with Xenophon's and Plato's Socrates that first fired my curiosity for philosophy. Some years later I read R. G. Collingwood's wonderful book *An Autobiography* and was humbled to read that he had already become familiar with the work of Kant before he had begun his philosophical studies at University, indeed even before he had gone to preparatory school.

> My father had plenty of books, and allowed me to read them as I pleased. Among others, he had kept the books of classical scholarship, ancient history and philosophy which he had used at Oxford. As a rule I left these alone; but one day when I was eight years old curiosity moved me to take down a little black book lettered on its spine "Kant's Theory of Ethics." It was Abbott's translation of the *Grundledung zur Metaphysik der Sitten*; and as I began reading it, my small form wedged between the bookcase and the table, I was attacked by a strange succession of emotions. First came an intense excitement. I felt that things of the highest importance were being said about matters of the utmost urgency; things which at all costs I must understand. Then, with a wave of indignation, came the discovery that I could not understand them. . . . Then, third and last, came the strangest emotion of all. I felt that the contents of this book,

although I could not understand it, were somehow my business:
a matter personal to myself, or rather to some future self of my
own. . . . I did not, in any natural sense of the word, "want" to
master the Kantian ethics when I should be old enough; but I
felt as if a veil had been lifted and my destiny revealed.[1]

Humbled though I was to read this I recognized the kind of
challenge which I had encountered. I too knew that in some way my
destiny had been revealed. I had found a way of looking at things, a call
to thinking, which was as intriguing as it was inevitable, as inevitable as
a vocation.

I cannot pretend that my university career as an Arts and later
Divinity undergraduate (those being the days of Divinity studies pursued
only after an initial degree) was in any way a dramatic development of
the awakening I have described. The beauty of Logic bewitched me and
Psychology seemed to be so essentially the modern way of understanding
those problems in morals and religion that had puzzled one's forbears.
Yet underlying this there was, I think, that sense of Reality which had
at the outset shaped my mind and imagination; and, though there have
been times when I thought Kierkegaard was an albatross hung on my
neck, I must confess that the discovery of his work as the area of my life's
study was the flowering of that original sense. When I look back at that,
it is almost a particular moment that I recall. I was simply a youth, beginning his studies with the aim of qualifying as a minister. The intellectual
requirements were all too well known to me; but so too were the more
personal, spiritual qualities that were demanded by ministry. This was
indeed what would have motivated the great Puritan character who was
my minister to introduce me to Kierkegaard. In my study of Kierkegaard
I have become more and more aware of his admiration for—and indeed
indebtedness to—Kant. Like Kant he did not think that philosophy was
some kind of external trapping, "an adornment of life," to use Kant's
happy phrase. Rather it was something that related to the philosopher's
own very being. One cannot read Kant's noble essay "What Does It Mean
to Orient Oneself in Thinking?" without being aware of its echoes in the
very different style of Kierkegaard. Terminology may have changed but
for both thought was nothing if it was not thinking for oneself which, for
Kant, meant "seeking the supreme touchstone of truth in oneself." That
vision is a conviction that has not simply haunted me in my own efforts

1. R. G. Collingwood, *An Autobiography*, 8–9.

but has inspired me in my work as a teacher of philosophy—within theology as well as on its own.

This quasi-autobiographical introduction is meant to explain why it was that several years ago when I was invited to deliver a series of lectures in the University of Wales, Bangor, I thought it might be profitable to argue for and possibly demonstrate the usefulness of Theology. These and the Southwell Lecture retain their original form, though the argument is updated: otherwise they would lose their sense of occasion. Some years previously the Arts Faculty to which I belonged in the University of Nottingham had been visited by a group of local members of Parliament and much of the talk had been about the *use* which could be made of various subjects. The politicians readily agreed that languages could be useful for the businessman and were even ready to admit that the cultural history of Europe could have some relevance and application. So the discussion proceeded until they turned to my neighbor, the Professor of Philosophy. His comments were terse. "Philosophy is of no earthly use at all," he said, and, indicating me, he continued, "It is not even of some eternal use like Theology." What I want to show is that Theology is of *temporal* as well as eternal use and that it has light to shed on problems that concern us and guidance to offer us in our perplexities as we live out our lives in this world. One of the saddest pieces of linguistic degradation or defamation that we have seen is the way in which politicians especially—particularly when they want to be abusive—refer to the discussions as "theological." What they mean is that such are as abstruse and ridiculously technical as the hoary example of controversy, viz "How many angels can stand on the point of a needle?" That is, they suggest that these are irrelevant discussions: concerned with some ideal eternal world perhaps they would have meaning but they are of no earthly use and in that sense meaningless. My contention, however, is that as theology begins with living religion, the life of faith lived in the real world, so it ends in that strengthening of faith as purposive living which is the great boon of understanding. In her now classical studies of Anselm's work Gillian Evans has shown the saint's remarkable contribution to both university and church as he taught us that faith seeks understanding and that nothing less than this is the goal of theology.

Wales has shown a strange ambivalence towards Theology. As a nation we rightly pride ourselves on our religious history and heritage, agreeing with the poet Gwenallt when he says that here the Holy Spirit was able to make a nest for himself. We remember with pride and perhaps nostalgia the halcyon days of the Sunday School as an institution. Yet, ancient as Welsh religious history is, it can hardly be said to boast an equal tradition of theological writing that is to be seen as part of the history of European theology. Nor has it fostered an intellectual tradition of theological study in the way that Charlemagne's work created a tradition in Paris. To say this is not to be unmindful of the many instances of significant theology which is our heritage: on the contrary, it is seeing that heritage for what it is. I think of the rather devastating way in which early Welsh philosophical and theological scholarship is viewed by a scholar such as John Marenbon. In his *From the Circle of Alcuin to the School of Auxerre* he highlighted the large complex of problems that contextualized the controversy over universals as a concern stretching all the way back to Aristotle's *Categories*. His Appendix 3 discusses glosses to the *Categoriae Decem* and in his treatment of ninth- and early tenth-century manuscripts to *Bern C 219*. This, he says, is a manuscript from Wales and then he says:

> If B is used as evidence of the Welsh roots of the English cultural renaissance at the time of the 10th Century then the picture which it supplies of the level of interest in logic is unflattering.[2]

The contribution of those churchmen who pioneered Welsh religious writing is wonderful; but this was literature and not theology so that even thirteenth-century texts such as the Red Book of Talgarth are hardly systematic theological writing. Rich beyond measure in theological content as Williams Pantycelyn's hymns are and learned as his *Pantheologia* is even here at the height of the Methodist Revival there is no theological endeavor. The obvious indebtedness of *Golwg ar Deyrnas* to Derham's Physico-Theology would suggest that Williams' theological thinking was derivative. Recently one has been reminded that the torrent of theological controversy in the nineteenth century produced some distinguished work such as that of R. S. Thomas. What is perhaps very telling is that he would still be a forgotten figure had not Professor Densil Morgan given us such a sympathetic picture of his genius in his delightfully informative *O'r Pwll Glo i Princeton : Bywyd a Gwaith R.S. Thomas, Abercynon, 1844–1928*. If my remarks seem to paint a rather jaundiced picture of Welsh cultural history perhaps it is useful to reflect that it took the University of Wales a whole century to integrate the Faculty

2. John Marenbon, *From the Circle of Alcuin to the School of Auxerre*, 177f.

of Theology within its College structure and until the latter part of the twentieth century theological study was confined within biblical studies.

What we know as biblical study was in fact part of what was once called biblical *theology*. The remarkable advances in specialist study of biblical text and history have tended to blind us to the ideal of reflection that inspired the earliest mediaeval critical study of the Bible. The essentially theological context of biblical study is something of which I could not but be aware, old enough as I am to remember the exciting aftermath of what was called in the 1930s "The New Theology." That liberation of theology from a narrowly confining orthodoxy was very largely the work of those theologians who had seen the message of the Bible in the light of the new method of biblical criticism and in relation to a developing knowledge and understanding of the world. The very achievement of biblical criticism as a purely technical apparatus could be said to reflect that advance in *theological* thinking whereby a text was released from an alien control. These gains, which were won by hard effort, put every living theologian in debt to an attitude which can only be described as liberal. This is why I strongly feel the necessity of theology's concern with the issues that occupy the minds and hearts of countless people in our society.

As a scholar, I have spent much of my time and energy working on the thought of Søren Kierkegaard. What I have learned from him is not easy to explain; but of the many lessons the one that stands out so clearly is the hollowness of any pretension by either a philosopher or theologian to be outside existence. We are creatures of time and it is with life's concerns that any proper thinking must be concerned. A privilege for which I shall never cease to be grateful is that I was taught by someone else who recognized his debt to Kierkegaard, Paul Tillich, one of the three or four really great theologians of the twentieth century. He used to say that theology was a study that answers questions; and when he described his *Systematic Theology* and his theological system as "a help in answering the questions . . . asked by people inside and outside churches"[3] he expressed the purpose of his system without any mock modesty. Though there must be problems for theological thought posed by the very nature of that eternity in which God dwells—not to mention all those problems that concern the Godhead itself—theology is, for the most part, given its questions by life itself. It was this very awareness that made Tillich insist

3. Paul Tillich, *Systematic Theology*, vol. 1, x

that theology was a boundary-science. This understanding of his life-work had a clarity that had been won only at the cost of great intellectual struggle and personal suffering. Committed to be a Christian thinker he had endured the pain of his work as a chaplain in World War I, been fired with the zeal for social reform that inspired post-war political thought, and had taken a first step towards formulating his system by a self-conscious attempt to see theology in relation to "the system of the sciences."

Though he had already passed the age of promise (born in 1886 and dying in 1965) he was, as I recall, at the end of his life full of extraordinary intellectual vigor and mental youthfulness so that in many ways he was still only in his prime. My memory of him in that last summer of his life is of someone who was fully engaged in the work he saw as incomplete. The third volume of *Systematic Theology* had been published and its faults weighed on him. His publishers wanted him to oversee the appearance of a complete English edition of his work. He, however, could not let go of the recently published work and he charged me with the task of letting him know of every page of Volume 3 where he did not say clearly what he meant and what, in my view, should be said. Fifteen years after the appearance of Volume 1 his "younger friends," he said, could assist him in his task. I am convinced that when the history of twentieth-century theology is written Tillich will be recognized as the main inspiration for what might be called a theology engaged with life in the real world. In the discussions that follow such is the theology I see raised by vital problems in medicine and ecology, not forgetting that life's end is a problem one must face and one's departure a problem for those who remain so that life's end is a complex problem of how to live. "Divinity," said Luther, "consists in use and practice not in speculation. Everyone that deals in speculation either in household affairs or temporal government, without practice, is lost and worth nothing."[4] And again, with typical force, he says that "true theology is practical . . . speculative theology belongs with the devil in hell."[5] To appreciate the truth underlying the hyperbole of the remarks one need only recall the subtlety of Luther's own argument in *De Babylonica Captivitate* where logic and metaphysics are put to good use in the argument about wrong practice. To see this is to understand the deep reciprocity between theoretical theology and practice. Theological

4. Luther, *Table Talk*, 179.
5. Luther, *W A*, 1, No. 153.

understanding can and does lead to action; but more significant is the way in which it can arise out of practice and be tested by practice. In *The Alternative Future* Roger Garaudy speaks of "the active nature of knowledge"[6] and such indeed is theological knowledge. Unlike both Plato and Aristotle the Christian theologian cannot give *theoria* superiority over *praxis*. Luther's theology of the cross is illuminating here—he saw the *via crucis* as embracing and transcending the *vita contemplative* and the *vita activa*.

J. Heywood Thomas,
Bonvilston, Vale of Glamorgan.

6. Roger Garaudy, *The Alternative Future*, 89.

Chapter 1

Theology and Matters of Life and Death

The words of the Psalmist that the lines had fallen to him in pleasant places express my own feelings on the good fortune of my being the successor of so many distinguished occupants of Nottingham's Chair of Christian Theology.[1] This is not the place nor am I the man to pay a proper tribute to them and their several contributions to the life of the University, to scholarship, and indeed to British culture. However, it would be remiss indeed of me were I not to seize the opportunity of paying at least a token tribute to the work of my immediate predecessor, Professor A. R. C. Leaney. His scholarship was typical of the tradition of biblical criticism that has been one of the great contributions of British theology—minute, careful study used as the basis of a fine understanding of the Bible. What is interesting to observe is that during the early 1970s, the years of greatest change in English theology since 1900, the chair was occupied by this scholar whose researches in the New Testament were uncovering its links with late Judaism. I want to point to this as something of a parable. The days of biblical theology are passed because it has given way to a new and, in a way, a more philosophical understanding of the historicity of religion. I am not belittling this tradition of theology, which dominated English academic theology for so long. On the contrary, I am just old enough to remember the exciting after-math of what was called in the 30s The New Theology. The liberation of theology from the bondage of a narrow and dogmatic outlook was very largely the work of those theologians who turned to the study of the Bible in the light of the new method of biblical criticism. This is a gain that those theologians

---

1. The Inaugural Lecture of the Chair of Christian Theology, Nottingham, delivered on 15th January 1976.

1

fought hard to secure and every theologian now—irrespective of his allegiance to any school, party, or church—is in their debt. This new liberal outlook has become the permanent heritage of theology. However, though evolution's law may be the preservation of balance its result is undoubtedly change. The very preoccupation of theology with the historical and literary study of the Bible has undergone an evolutionary development into something that can be called a more comprehensive and synoptic study. The treatment of the Bible as a piece of literature spawned work on semantics and the very structure and purpose of the writings. As discussion of text, form, and meaning took note of sociological thought so the historical study of biblical content enlarged and transformed the cognate study, comparative religion, into the phenomenological and multi-faceted study that religious studies is today.

What I have to say can be stated quite simply, though it may be very difficult for me to expound and argue it. I want to say that theology is concerned with questions about life and death and that as such it is a study that is, as Paul Tillich used to say, on the boundary with other subjects. I shall have something to say later about what I have learned from my study of Tillich and Kierkegaard, but let me suggest that when the history of twentieth-century theology comes to be written it will be because of his vision of theology as a borderline study that Tillich will be seen as one of that very small band of really great theologians. There are several ways in which his fulfilment of his own aim has left some unfinished business for contemporary theology. There is, for instance, his concern for a theology of healing where the theologian faces not only the difficult problems created by the increasing use of psychological categories in our everyday language but also the thorny problems raised by advances in medical technology and by a widening of the notion of healing. There is also the boundary with politics and sociology where Tillich showed himself more aware than any other theologian of our day of the necessity for the Christian church to stand in a dialectical relationship with Marxism. For it is remarkable that in a world where Marxism is perhaps the most powerful single intellectual force and could even perhaps ironically be described in Marx's own terms as a bourgeois ideology English-speaking theologians have seemed unaware of its existence. Finally, I would mention Tillich's unique work as a theologian of culture. It is true that with an abstraction that was typically German he concentrated on the relation of theology to philosophy, but, even so, he did raise for us the problem of the relation between theology and all expressions of culture.

Let me begin my argument by saying something about biblical theology. It will, I think, be agreed by historians of Christian thought that the concept was originally formulated as a slogan of reform. In his erudite paper *The Meaning of "Biblical Theology"* Gerhard Ebeling quotes Spener as evidence for saying that the concept was not a criticism of either the content of orthodox dogmatics or of its form as systematic theology. Rather, it was a criticism of the adulteration of theology by the accretions it had gathered. He quotes Spener as saying that much had been "introduced into theology which is alien, useless and savours more of the wisdom of the world . . . presumptuous subtleties in matters whereof we ought not to be wise above the Scriptures." "The whole of Theologia must therefore be brought back to the apostolic simplicity," to the true "simplicity of Christ and his teaching."[2] Thus the slogan of a biblical theology was the call not for a creation of something different from systematic theology but for the reform of systematic theology itself. However, what was thus originally merely a criticism of the scholastic form of theology soon became a demand for a rival kind of theology[3] and it was impossible to call a halt to this development. As Ebeling puts succinctly it,[4] that development was dominated by self-contradictory tendencies. Biblical theology rejected any directives for its own work from dogmatics but it was obliged to claim the respect of dogmatics and in fact was guided by a strong dogmatic interest. Ebeling's masterly analysis of the history of the concept clearly shows, I think, how biblical theology as it developed carried within it the seeds of its own destruction. What brings that about is the modern interest in the methodology and conceptual framework of theology. Therefore, it seems to me that an opposition between biblical and systematic theology is false.

There is a very obvious sense in which the programme of biblical theology is dubious whether it is the theology of the whole Bible or of only one or other of the Testaments. I am not here discussing the problem of specialization. My objection is based not on such pragmatic considerations but on a logical point. Even if we had a polymath, a modern Erasmus, who could cover the whole area of biblical scholarship

2. Gerhard Ebeling, *Word and Faith*, 84f.

3. Ibid., 87.

4. Ibid., 88–89.

it does not follow that what he is able to produce is a biblical theology. What is described as theology is in fact at best a history of theology and at worst a history of religious ideas. If we assume for a moment that such a thing as the theology of the New Testament is possible then this means that the theology of John and the theology of Paul are one and the same thing. This clearly is not the case. Further, it can be objected that this use of the term "theology" is an example of our tendency to confuse the terms "religion" and "theology." I shall return to this point later; but for the moment what matters is that very often when we mean to refer to a man's religious convictions we talk of his theology. The furthest thing from our mind in such usage is that there is any sophistication of either belief or argument involved. Thus it is a confusing use of the term, suggesting a continuity between the ideas of religion and the concepts of theology that does not exist. I am not arguing for a separation of theology from religious faith but merely pointing out that it cannot be the case that an essential part of religion is sophistication of either its ideas or argument.

The other aspect of the confusion of religion with theology concerns the comparative study of religion. In a most perceptive and illuminating article published in *Religious Studies* Professor Zwi Werblowsky argues for a symbolic understanding of religions as systems of meaning and makes the point that this raises a problem about what is called *theologia religionum*.[5] The student of comparative religion operates from a point outside religion no matter what religious commitment he may make as an individual believer. The theologian, on the other hand, argues Werblowsky, must operate from within a religious system.

> Trying to give a reasoned account of their faith, theologians have to consider all relevant aspects of reality, and this reality includes the fact of the existence of "other" religions. Hence theologians must formulate what their respective religions believe not only about God, the soul, salvation, etc., but also about the other religions. They all have, explicitly or implicitly, a "theology of religions." What all these have in common is that each view, articulated from within a particular tradition, assumes its own religion to be the summit and apex of the pyramid.[6]

5. Werblowsky, "On Studying Comparative Religion," 145–56.
6. Ibid., 152.

His comments on this phenomenon are various. First, he contends that this kind of study reflects a philosophical judgment about other religions rather than a genuine understanding of their specificity and certainly it is not a matter of empirical investigation and generalization of the results. Secondly, he characterizes this study as theological in its orientation and here the term theological seems to me to imply a certain authoritarian definition of meaning. Thus he says that the orientation is evident in the long catalogue of books and articles whose titles begin "Christianity and . . .," "Judaism and . . .," etc. That is, the assumption is that there is only one norm of religious meaning and the facts of religion are to be surveyed with reference to that. Professor Werblowsky refers to the contemporary eirenical mood of scholars but adds that this kind of development does not change the essential nature of the perspective.

> The ultimate imperialism of even the most profoundly generous ecumenical mind is well illustrated by William Temple: "All that is noble in the non-Christian systems of thought, or conduct, or worship is the work of Christ upon them and within them." An extremely sophisticated version of this doctrine is presented by Raymond Panikkar; e.g. *The Unknown Christ of Hinduism* (1964), or *The Trinity and the Religious Experience of Man* (1970). After reading about the "unknown Christ of Hinduism" all one can do is to wait for a Mahayana Buddhist to write on the unknown Buddha of Christianity. Sooner or later the point is reached where even theologians have to ask themselves whether they wish to be taken seriously or whether they are engaged in inventing new variations of the old Humpty Dumpty game.[7]

What I have said about biblical theology has served to show how theology, even at its most empirical, must be speculative. This was one of the fundamental lessons I learnt from Tillich. It was not so much that he was seen as a speculative theologian because he created one of the two or three systems of theology that the modern world has seen but that his whole output since the celebrated 1919 lecture on the theology of culture was an attempt to fulfil a speculative task. Characteristically he thus met a need of theology that he did not state except by implication. It seems to me that the real interest of biblical theology was its preoccupation with historical method and it is ironic that the development of historical studies of religion is what finally killed it. Be that as it may, it was surely the conviction that we were able to found a theology on the facts of history

7. Ibid.

that was the attraction of biblical theology. Therefore, the interest of biblical theology and its relevance as a theological methodology was that it offered an answer to the basic philosophical problem of how we know the truth of the theological claims. It is a further irony that the popularity of biblical theology reflects the death of the old-fashioned idealism that dominated British philosophy and theology until 1920 and the consequent neglect of philosophy by theology. Though Tillich condemned the practice of modern philosophy to reduce all questions to epistemology he himself offered in *Systematic Theology* vol. II such a philosophical validation of the cliché of biblical theology that we do not have a biographical account of Jesus in the New Testament evidence. It is clear that without such work the whole effort of biblical criticism produces for theology nothing more than castles in the air.

There is, however, a more fundamental matter of theology that seems to me to reveal the speculative character of theology. Discussing Professor Werblowsky's paper I mentioned that he saw religion as a scheme of symbols bearing meaning. This reminds me that throughout his writings Tillich emphasized the importance of the concept of meaning for understanding religion. I am not here concerned to expound Tillich's work, but it can be justly said that one of the remarkable features of his work is the combination of a new scientific understanding of religion with both a sensitive sociological understanding of his world and a passionate concern for Christian communication. He tells us that he was painfully aware that after 1918 "the whole house was in ruins." Like Marx before him he condemned the Christian church of his day with the authentic voice of a prophet; and when he represented the Christian faith to his contemporaries he did this in a very Marxist way. Without ever trying to dissociate man from the world to which he is tied Tillich describes religion as the experience of the absolute—that is, man's ultimate meaning and the basis of his meaning. This is not to look outside the world for this reality of meaning any more than it is a matter of identifying it with the world. Tillich deliberately rejected the description of religion in terms of a relation to a supernatural object called God because he felt that this was a misleading way of expressing its revelation of ultimate meaning. At the very heart of man's existential situation then, Tillich argues, is man's quest for meaning. In this way, too, I should want to see theology as concerned with the speculative problem of the meaning of existence.

To talk about meaning is at once to be in dialogue with philosophy, and there is a real danger that the theologian engages in a diatribe against rather than a dialogue with the philosopher. Even now there is a great deal of nonsense talked by theologians about linguistic philosophy. The great temptation for theology is that of canonizing old-fashioned and therefore moribund philosophies. I have myself argued that linguistic analysis is a necessary part of theology; but it would be quite wrong to argue that this is an exhaustive account of the method to be employed in philosophy of religion. Even so, if method it is then we must say that it cannot be elevated into some doctrine of meaning. It is thus perfectly possible to avoid a narrow and doctrinaire empiricism that would maintain that the question "What is the meaning of existence?" is a meaningless question. That it is a speculative question rather than a merely practical problem seems to me worth emphasizing because the ready recognition by the theologian of its practical character tempts us to construe the question as nothing more. It was said by more than one person who survived the horrors of Nazi concentration camps that they were able to endure their suffering because it meant their active struggle against the evil of Hitler's regime. Tillich once told me that he felt his own work as a teacher of theology had been worthwhile when he was told by a former pupil that it was the recollection of that teaching which had enabled the young man to endure the agony of the concentration camp. Obviously the theologian wants to stress the practical dimension of faith. The noble army of martyrs praise God, says the Te Deum, and we pray that we should praise Him not only with our lips but in our lives. The Westminster Confession makes the point with characteristic economy, saying that man's chief end is to glorify God and enjoy Him forever. There is good reason, then, for wanting to stress the practical interest of the question; but equally, I feel, there can be no doubt that questions such as "Why is there a world at all?" form part of the question of the meaning of existence and that these are clearly speculative. It would be idle as it would be foolish of me to claim that I am inaugurating a new development in theology in the way in which Kant in his Inaugural Dissertation of 1770 outlined the prolegomena to any future metaphysic. Yet though I cannot in the same way claim that this preceding year has been my year of great light it has become increasingly clear to me that my task as a theologian is not only speculative but inescapable and inevitable. When I say that it is an inevitable task I mean more than that it is a natural function of human reason. It was, I think, one of Kierkegaard's great achievements that he both understood this point that Kant had made about metaphysics and went further in his own understanding of it. In *Philosophical Fragments* he portrays the condition of human reason as that foolhardiness of passion that pushes it forward to its own destruction. The end of reason's quest is the Paradox. The inevitability of the theological task is born of the fact that there is here a congruence of human quest for and the divine revelation of the meaning of existence. The basic significance of religious assertions is their truth and the clear implication of the truth of the assertion that God's goodness is absolute is that the universe is, as F. C. S. Schiller said, friendly.

The claim of Christianity that the meaning of life is disclosed in the life, death, and resurrection of a Jewish carpenter is not a practical statement or a historical assertion. It is not indeed a dialectical conclusion so that St. Ambrose could well say (and Newman could embellish the title page of *The Grammar of Assent* with the saying) it did not please God to save us by dialectic. Yet speculative or metaphysical this certainly is, as is indeed the very understanding of the nature of history that it contains. In his immensely learned work *The Grand Design of God* Dr. C. A. Patrides has shown very clearly how crucial a theme for the whole history of Western thought and English literature in particular is the Christian view of history. The detail of his evidence gives clear confirmation of Karl Lowith's contention in his book *Meaning in History* that the idea of progress is the secularized version of the Christian doctrine of providence. The idea of progress had no place in Greek thought, where the model adopted for understanding nature and life was a circle rather than a line. Probably the only exception is the difficulty raised by Aristotle[8] concerning the measurement of time by the orbiting of the stars and this, as far as I know, was nowhere else discussed.[9] Linear thinking emerges with the christological and christocentric understanding of history in the New Testament.[10]

T. S. Eliot puts it memorably in "The Rock":

> Then came, at a predetermined moment, a moment in time and of time,
> a moment not out of time, but in time, in what we call history:
> transecting, bisecting the world of time, a moment in time
> but not like a moment of time.
> A moment of time but time was made through that moment:
> for without the meaning there is no time, and that moment of time

---

8. Aristotle, *Physics* Bk. IV 223 a 21ff.

9. See R. Weil, "Aristotle's View of History."

10. See, for instance, Oscar Cullman's *Christ and Time*, 51–60.

gave the meaning.[11]

It has been remarked by several critics that the Victorian legacy to twentieth-century thought of an obsession with time has resulted in dramatically different literary expressions.[12] I shall take only one example, which will also serve as a link with our next topic. This may strike some as a ludicrous example, but to my mind there is a marvellous profundity in the description of Lord Cut-Glass.

> Lord Cut-Glass, in his kitchen full of time, squats down alone to a dogdish, marked Fido, of peppery fish-scraps and listens to the voices of his sixty-six clocks, one for each year of his loony age, and watches, with love, their black-and-white moony loudlipped faces tocking the earth away. . . . His sixty-six singers are all set at different hours. Lord Cut-Glass lives in a house and a life at siege. Any minute or dark day now, the unknown enemy will loot and savage downhill, but they will not catch him napping.[13]

Dylan Thomas has not been sufficiently appreciated as a religious poet, though critical opinion fastened quite early on the startling echoes of Christian language in his imagery. No one can, however, deny that the concluding stanzas of Poem on his Birthday express a majestic and courageous resurrection faith:

> That the closer I move
> To death, one man through his sundered hulks,
> The louder the sun blooms
> And the tusked, ramshackling sea exults;
> and Every wave of the way
> And gale I tackle, the whole world then,
> With more triumphant faith
> Than ever was since the word was said,
> Spins its morning of praise, . . .
> . . . Oh,
> Holier then their eyes,
> And my shining men no more alone
> As I sail out to die.[14]

---

11. T. S. Eliot, *Complete Poems and Plays*, 107.

12. See the bibliographical riches of Dr. C. A. Patrides, *The Grand Design of God*, 138–39, n.36.

13. Dylan Thomas, *Under Milk Wood*, 65.

14. Dylan Thomas, *Miscellany Two*, 36.

This leads me to what I want to say next; namely that the question of the meaning of existence is as concerned with the meaning of death as it is with the meaning of life. Sociological accounts of twentieth-century attitudes to death will be of the utmost importance for the historian of religion. One may observe that it is a remarkable fact that as the general view of death has become more and more secularized there has been a corresponding growth of a taboo on the subject and indeed a deprecia-tion of the ritual of burial. I readily confess that if I may speak in this perplexing way I should prefer to witness my own funeral procession led by a carriage with two black horses, a not unfamiliar sight in my child-hood, than by the most opulent Rolls, Cadillac, or Mercedes. But I am not talking of foibles or personal taste when I say that the modern fu-neral, hedged around by widely shared taboos, is a refusal to value death. To turn from sociology to philosophy, it may have been Wittgenstein's intention to rule out of court questions about the experience of death when he said in the *Tractatus* that in death the world does not change but ceases, and that death is not an event in life.[15] However, what he said is so puzzling that he can well be credited with the distinction of being the one philosopher who has faced the problem of death, because this oracu-lar aphorism is like a signpost that leads away from itself in an opposite direction. When I say that Wittgenstein is the only philosopher to face this problem I mean, of course, the only one in *this* country, because we can find lengthy and illuminating discussions in the works of the existen-tialist philosophers and in the less well-known treatment of the theme in the work of Kierkegaard. Heidegger sees death as the end whereby man's existence becomes complete. Man's capacity to anticipate death, to see it as the context within which every moment falls, is the basis for any attempt to grasp his existence as an organic unity.[16] For Jaspers, too, death is the fulfilment of being, an occasion that can enable man to be most truly himself.[17] Sartre, however, will have none of this high valuation of death.[18] It is I, he says, who give my death meaning and not death which gives me meaning. All this is very instructive; for there is in existentialist philosophy a very clear understanding of the way in which metaphysical beliefs are determinative of human behavior. What these philosophers

15. Wittgenstein, *Tractatus Logico-Philosophicus*, 6.431, 6.4311.

16. Cf. Heidegger, *Being and Time*, 279–90.

17. Cf. Jaspers, *Philosophie*, ii, 220–29.

18. Cf. Sartre, *L'être et le néant*, 617–33.

tell us about death can be properly called the commendation of a particular policy of behavior, but not because it is something different from a metaphysical assertion about the meaning of death. This is where I see this discussion as making a contribution to both philosophy and theology. Whereas so much traditional metaphysics is concerned with establishing that a man shall live again after he dies these philosophers attend to the more immediate problem of what is meant by death itself. They did this, I believe, because they found in Kierkegaard an example not only of a general method that would imply such an approach but also an example of such a particular discussion. Indeed, I should argue that the insights of all the existentialist philosophers (even those of Sartre) are derived from Kierkegaard, that solitary Christian soul whose agonies in the nineteenth century were so prophetic and indeed determinative of twentieth-century thought. As well as the fugitive references to the subject in the *Journal* and in some of the works there is a lengthy discussion in *Concluding Unscientific Postscript,* which is so careful a piece of analysis of the various ways in which one talks of death that one might forget that it was written in 1845. For example, one can predict somebody's death, one can compose an elegy about somebody's death, or one can conduct a funeral service after someone's death: we still have not established a paradigm of what it is to understand death.

> I had better think about this, lest existence mock me, because I had become so learned and highfalutin that I had forgotten to understand what will sometime happen to me as to every human being—sometime, nay what am I saying: suppose death were so treacherous as to come tomorrow! Merely this one uncertainty, when it is to be understood and held fast by an existing individual, and hence enter into every thought, precisely because . . . I make it clear to myself whether if death comes tomorrow I am beginning upon something that is worth beginning—merely this one uncertainty generates inconceivable difficulties.[19]

Kierkegaard is saying two things about death. In the first place, there is a difficulty in this matter of understanding death, which is due merely to its uncertainty. Secondly, properly to understand death we must see that death is *my* death or *your* death. It is the second point that is the more important for him and consequently colors the first; but the two points are made. The unpredictability of death makes it the context

19. Kierkegaard, *Concluding Unscientific Postscript,* 148.

for any moment of human experience. Thus the supreme oblivion of the figure of Jesus in the Gospels to the threat of a totalitarian government, an occupying force, that could and would eradicate him is more than stoicism. The life that agonized in the Garden of Gethsemane was consistently lived in the context of that moment of time when he was on the threshold of eternity. As Teilhard de Chardin says, "The great victory of the creator and redeemer in the Christian vision is to have transformed what is in itself a universal power of diminishment and extinction into an essentially life-giving factor."[20]

A Christian theology of death will clearly take as its point of departure this memory of that death and the relation of Jesus' temporal existence up to that point to what followed. The identity of Jesus who is crucified with the Christ who is raised is a presupposition of the doctrine of redemption and eternal life. This may seem a very obvious point, but there is an interesting and not very obvious implication. As I have said, there is a relation of consistency between ante-mortem and post-mortem accounts of Jesus in the Gospels and what strikes me as interesting here is the relation of his temporal and non-temporal existence. Whatever we say about the resurrection it was not in any simple sense a temporal event, and it is not surprising that in the history of Christian apologetics the argument for immortality from the story of Jesus' three days' sojourn in the tomb has been very popular because we can see in the doctrine of Jesus' resurrection the way in which time and eternity are linked in the Christian faith. The particular point I want now to make concerns the ethical use of this metaphysics. To quote Kierkegaard once again, he contrasts the way in which the existing individual asks the question of immortality with the abstract way in which the Hegelian metaphysician does. "So [the existing individual] asks how he is to behave in order to express in existence his immortality."[21] Presenting Christianity, as he said, from the side of God there was nothing that Kierkegaard condemned so consistently and vehemently as that bourgeois confusion of Christianity with the values generally accepted by society or some such convenient tradition. In castigating this morality he made us aware of a deeper kind of morality, not what he calls a summary of police ordinances but more an imitation of the Pattern. Kierkegaard's view of Christianity is often described as an extreme asceticism and very often writers make free use

20. Teilhard de Chardin, *Le Milieu Divin*, 161.

21. Kierkegaard, *Postscript*, 157

of such easy and ambiguous adjectives as pathological and masochistic. To my mind the truth of the matter is that he gave full value to the metaphors that are familiar to us in the language of liturgy and Christian devotion—that we die to the world in order to be raised again to life in Christ, that we no longer live but Christ lives in us.

The second point that I mentioned in Kierkegaard's discussion is that the language of death is self-involving language. Death is mine, despite all Sartre's perfectly proper protests against the way in which romantic literature personalized death. A theology of death must be characterized by realism rather than romanticism. "I will die" is not a statement that can be exhaustively analyzed into statements about my body. So the problem of the meaning of death becomes the old problem of the nature of man, a problem that gains an urgency because the different views will yield different expectations of his destiny. When I say that it is impossible to reduce "I will die" to statements that are matters of publicly verifiable assertion, purely empirical meaning, I am not suggesting that we must regard man as a synthesis of two substances—body and soul. I am saying merely that "I will die" does not function in the same way as "This body will disappear." We are not talking of a series of events of which description could be given but of a series of events which taken together will disclose me to myself. No account of myself in terms of scientific discourse can be adequate; for it does not exhaust the subjectivity that is my self-awareness. One obvious point that was made by Wittgenstein's dictum that death is not an event in life is that I cannot say at any time in my life "I have died"; but there is a sense in which it is true to say "The body which was mine ten years ago has ceased to be" and an obvious sense in which we can refer to objects saying that such and such an object has ceased to exist. I cannot, that is, describe my death as an event in the world in the way in which things that occur are events in the world and even someone else's death, however much I am involved, is such an event. As Kierkegaard puts it,[22] one would have to be extremely absent-minded to imagine that you did not know that you were dead until you tried to get up. The fact of my own death is not such a something in general. The ethical point that Kierkegaard made is linked with the metaphysical one. Asking the question of immortality is for the existing individual a deed, an act. The attitude to death, then, is not merely something that colors the series of events which is my life: it

22. Ibid., 149.

13

is part of that series. Tillich approaches this kind of position in his little classic *The Courage to Be* when he says that there is in much contemporary culture an anxiety about death to which the only solution or cure is this ontological courage.[23]

It may be said that I am speaking very loosely here when I speak of the ethical dimension of the problem of death. That this is not so will be clear if we reflect that here once again Kierkegaard stands very close to Kant and echoes that same sense of the profound mystery of human freedom which Professor MacKinnon has reminded us is so characteristic of Kant.[24] Part of the mystery of man's freedom is his ability to sacrifice it, and it is precisely of that sacrifice and its opposite which I speak in this matter of the ethics of death. I find a startling example in the brilliant poem written by Sylvia Plath in the last week of her life.[25] I shall quote only part of "Edge":

> The woman is perfected,
> Her dead
> Body wears the smile of accomplishment,
> The illusion of a Greek necessity
> Flows in the scrolls of her toga,
> Her bare
> Feet seem to be saying
> We have come so far, it is over.[26]

Calling this a pathological attitude does not help. The wisest comment is that of A. Alvares: "Poetry of this kind is a murderous art."[27] It is an example of a determined rather than a free attitude to death. Talk of the analogical nature of a religious language is a commonplace but here is an area that is perhaps too little noticed. Not only in Paul's letters but in the whole homiletic tradition and in the classics of spirituality there is a very important analogical use of the language of death. What makes it important is the ontological basis of the analogy, something perceived by the now largely forgotten von Hugel in his *Essays and Addresses*.[28]

---

23. Tillich, *The Courage to Be*, 40 et passim.
24. Cf. D. M. MacKinnon, *A Study in Ethical Theory*.
25. Ted Hughes, "Notes on the Chronological Order of Sylvia Plath's Poems," 195.
26. Sylvia Plath, *Ariel*, 85.
27. A. Alvares, *Art of Sylvia Plath*, 67.
28. von Hugel, *Essays and Addresses*, Vol. 2, 227–28.

I have spoken of various matters of life and death on which theology seems to me to have something to say. In the course of the discussion it has become clear that in so doing theology moves on the borders of such fields as philosophy, literature, politics, and sociology. This may be clear enough evidence of that combination of practical and speculative interest of which I spoke earlier. But let me end this lecture by taking as an example a border area that cannot fail to illustrate the way in which theology is a borderline study that transcends the distinction between theory and practice—I refer to the area of medical ethics. Clinically induced death, whether of unborn children or of ailing elderly patients or incurable patients, is a subject that has been very much in the news. This is a complex subject which easily and quickly illustrates the importance of philosophical and theological discussion of matters of life and death and not simply of a code of practice. In both cases there is a pressing need for clear definition of life and death. When does the foetus become a person? When has a person died? When does physical existence cease to merit the term "life"? Already we can see how the old issue of the soul, which we have once before mentioned in this lecture, comes to the fore-front of our discussion. Indeed the theological problem is the self same problem as that which confronts the medical practitioner as he decides his course of action. One reason, then, for coupling the problem of abor-tion with that of euthanasia is that the logical and metaphysical prob-lems are basically the same. The nature of the ethical choices is also very much alike. Therefore, I want to take the much less controversial problem of transplant surgery. We are not clear in our minds—whether we are doctors, priests, theologians, or laymen—about either the practice of transplant surgery or the kind of legislation needed to promote good medical care yet also protect the rights of the individual; but most of us take a favorable view of it. Assuming that the obvious problems are answered satisfactorily why do we still feel some slight hesitation about giving our consent to a transplant operation? Is this feeling for the hu-man remains an expression of a true insight that cannot be disregarded? There seems to be no obvious theological reason for viewing a corpse as in any sense sacred. It is the living body that is what the apostle calls the temple of the Spirit, and it would be naïve indeed to imagine that there is any connection between the treatment of a corpse and the expectation of the resurrection of the body. Yet it seems to me that we cannot treat a human corpse as merely a piece of scrap. On the contrary, it must be treated in the full recognition that not even the death that this body has suffered removes the person from the presence of God. Therefore, we cannot speak of that person except as a person. Similarly we cannot treat the token of the person's presence with anything less than respect. In the history of religion there are two kinds of considerations to be seen at work in the practices associated with death. One is that certain things must be done as part of the proper ongoing life of the society. The other is that certain things must be done because they are duties towards the departed. Socrates' death is a very good example of this. Socrates probably, if we are to take Plato's picture of him as our guide, viewed death as a release from the body: and characteristically he said to Crito immediately before he died, "I owe a cock to Asclepius: do not forget it." To which Crito replied, "It will be done." (*Phaedo*, cf. *Euthyphro*, *Apology* and *Crito*). Socrates' obligations towards his friends had been discharged and he is here putting upon Crito an obligation towards him, an obligation which Crito accepts gladly. To return to our problem, the fundamental question with regard to transplants is whether the body of the person who has died in some sense belongs to him any more. Socrates was not asking Crito to bury him in any particular way; but had he done so the obligation would have been just as clear as the liturgical one. If someone says that he does not wish his body to be used for transplant surgery we should generally say that this wish should be respected. But if there is no specific obligation does it follow that there is no obligation at all? I am not in any way arguing against the use of bodies for transplant surgery. What I want to make clear is that the respect we feel for a body is based on its recognition as a token of the person's presence and that the basis for that is the Christian belief in the solidarity of the human race before God. This is the basis that makes Professor Paul Ramsey argue in a most polemical but illuminating way that there are limits beyond which medical practice should not go.[29] Though the body is indeed not sacred it has made possible that personal act which is death and as such it is the symbol of that person's moral value. This is why I do not think that moral philosophy gives an adequate account of obligation to the dead. Mr. J. D. Mabbot has well shown[30] that the act-utilitarian account does not give any reason for fulfilling an obligation to someone who is dead. What we need is some guarantee of this being properly seen as an interpersonal relation. It is because I think that theology can illumine our understanding of such

29. Ramsey, *Fabricated Man*, and *Patient as Person*.
30. Mabbot, "Moral Rules," 211.

ordinary human experience that I suggest that it has relevance for the moral problems of medical practice.

Philosophy was once known as the handmaid of theology. To my mind it always will shape, as it always has shaped, theology. But we have reached a period in the history of theology when we need to echo the kind of ecumenicity that Dante gives his Christ when the ancient heroes too are given their place in paradise by the Son of Man. So to the sociologist, the poet, the literary critic, the political theorist, as well as to the philosopher I would extend an invitation to lend me their aid as I undertake *ministerium verbi divini*, the theologian's task of the service of the Word of God.

Chapter 2

The Problem of the Unborn Life

Few issues have brought the marketplace into the sanctum of theology so persistently and often violently as that of the unborn life. There are times when modern advances in medicine strike the man in the street as something akin to the fantasies of television. Yet the reports in the media of what has in fact been done or is about to be done medically make him either recoil in horror at the thought of what he sees as a technologically produced bionic man or applaud the way in which we are now able to subdue nature to make our dreams reality. Either way theologians tend to be drawn into the argument. Thus it may be protested that some particular medical advance is a case of doctors playing at being God, something that the theologian should therefore unequivocally condemn. On the other hand, the reaction may be that theological sanctions stand in the way of progress, a development that is not simply wonderful but likewise beneficent. For the latter reaction technological possibilities now confronting doctors are self-justifying, enabling medical procedures hitherto only dreamt of and many laymen are only too ready to point to possible benefits. To others the possibility of the technology just as much as the procedure it enables takes us into the realm of action that is either definitely prohibited or at any rate undesirable. So once again appeal is made to theology for a resolution of the conflict. This simple recognition of the way in which conflicting attitudes raise issues of theological justification is no indication of the emotion that any question concerning the unborn life will raise so that it is little wonder that the problem has been at the forefront of theological discussion in the marketplace; and the continuing advance of medicine makes it all the more obvious and pressing. Already there is a host of well-established possibilities in our treatment of unborn life which are of such pressing urgency that we need more specific guidance than the vague theories that for the man in the street constitute theology.

Can theology provide specific guidance and not simply the wisdom of general counsels? What is very clear is that theology and ethics cannot be separated any more than faith and morals can. In the 1930s the need to clarify the relation was recognized by J. H. Oldham who advocated what has been known as the middle-axiom approach. Between the doctrines of theology and the definition of Christian principles Oldham and those who followed his approach saw there were such axioms that were, by their nature, less general than the bases and were the grounds on which definite policies of social action were justified. While such mapping of the basis for the provision of moral guidance in the light of Christian belief is a necessary corrective to gloomy predictions of the over-weaning pride of technological man, such as C. S. Lewis' moral tale, *The Hideous Strength*, it leaves both the justifying argument and the nature of the policies themselves unclear. Butler's view of conscience as the criterion of right and wrong is an example of this mapping out of particular moral activity. Thus in Sermon XII he says that though the good of creation is indeed God's purpose in creation yet we may have particular obligations that we can appreciate without being able to see the connection between the general principle and these particular duties. It is significant that doctors often bewail the lack of guidance they are given by the public at large and especially by those who formally represent religious opinion. A clear example of the way in which law leaves very often a grey area of moral confusion is the aftermath of the UK's Warnock Report of 1984 in connection with the problem of surrogacy. Any assisted surrogate motherhood was to be forbidden and contracts for surrogacy should be unenforceable in law but not banned altogether. What is worth noting is that the grounds for objecting were twofold: it was inconsistent with human dignity and distorted bonding. In so far as such thinking was clearly worked out it was concerned with some notion of an unborn life, a concept that could easily be interpreted as theological, the indeterminate nature of created life in terms of time. That is to say, one could not set any limit on the reach of God's creative action. This would seem to be the thought behind the Catholic objections. Paragraph 11 of the Catholic Bishops' Response speaks of the "interests of . . . the new human being"; Paragraph 16 points to the "evil of seeing human beings as products"; and

Paragraph 19 brings out the notion most clearly when it speaks of the rights of the unborn life.

What I have said about the confusion that was seen in so much thinking after the Warnock Report might be construed as a complaint that the Report did not broach these theological issues I have raised. That, however, would be to criticize the Committee quite unfairly. It will be clear from what I said concerning middle-axioms that the Committee quite properly concentrated on the moral and purely moral issues concerning *in vitro* fertilization, asking then what moral principles should govern the treatment of a human embryo. However, while recognizing the autonomy of morals the theologian cannot ignore the relevance of theological vision to the domain of ethics and particularly to the place of morality in public action. Equally any theologian aware of the advance of medical research and practice is all too keenly aware of the entirely new problems posed by the unborn life. Already there are a host of well-established possibilities in our treatment of unborn life that are of such pressing urgency that we need more specific guidance than the general counsels that are so often the sum of theological wisdom. Gloomy predictions of the over-weaning pride of technological man—such as C. S. Lewis gave in his moral tale, *That Hideous Strength*—is only one half of the prophetic message, the other half being, as always, the mapping of moral guidance in the light of man's creative responsibility, which for Christian ethics gains special force through the doctrine of Incarnation. The way in which law leaves a grey area of moral confusion was the aftermath of the Warnock Report. The issue of surrogacy was tackled in the UK's Surrogacy Arrangements Act of July 1985—only to leave private and non-profit-making agencies legal. So neither the politicians nor the public had given much thought to the new problems, which, by the very novelty of the information and understanding presupposed, were very difficult. If we return to the Report we can see how the theologian cannot ignore this kind of problem by considering the reason given for its moral objection to surrogacy—"That people should treat others as a means to their own ends, however desirable the consequences, must always be liable to moral objection" (*Report*. Para. 8). On reading this, the theologian would be reminded of Kant's Categorical Imperative and also of the dominical injunction that we love our neighbor as ourselves. What seems to me remarkable about so much Christian moral thought is that, apart from Kierkegaard, little attention has been given to the concept of loving *oneself*, which is the basis of that comparative definition of Christian duty. How does one love oneself? Where in such love does one distinguish between means and ends? This is indeed an example of the way in which apparently simple Christian moral injunctions turn out to be rather complex. I raise the issue not to pursue the matter further but simply to show that theology does impinge on moral discussion despite our recognition that there is no *a priori* definition of moral content.

In her account[1] of her activity as Chairman of the Committee on Human Fertilization and Embryology Dame Mary Warnock makes very clear that what perhaps induced her to accept the responsibility was the moral and philosophical issues arising in this moral context. With her humane approach as a philosopher, Dame Mary was interested in the theoretical relationship between morality and law and was very much aware of the philosophical issues that would arise in discussing unborn life. She would have appreciated that in so much of our thinking on the subject there is an unexamined assumption that we not only know what "life" is but are also able to form clear and strict moral guidelines by means of that concept. Thus in relation to the discussion of abortion the theological argument might be that we have an absolute duty to pre-serve and protect life because it is a gift of God and that our life is in God's hands. Consequently, it would be argued, no interference with the development of unborn life is justified. Confronting this argument several things need to be said. First, it should be noticed that the doctrine of creation is used in two different ways—creation is seen as the source of the "gift" and then creation is seen as limiting any notion of human responsibility for human life. The conflation of the arguments thus makes clear very different moral considerations. Thus, that my life is a gift from God does not *of itself* imply that it is not my possession as is claimed in the oft-expressed argument—"My life is my own." In relation to abortion this latter point might be said to have less force; but we are not free of difficulty in the second case either. To say that life is in God's hands does not entail that there can be no case for human intervention. The very story of creation in Genesis envisages not only the propriety but indeed the *need* for human intervention in creation. Adam tends the garden and the man and wife beget children.[2] The argument baldly stated and rigidly argued would lead to the nonsensical position that no action could claim justification, let alone the difficult case of intervening in the development

1. Mary Warnock, *Nature and Mortality*, Continuum, 69, 73 et passim.
2. Gen 2; 4.

of the unborn life. However, the crucial point is that the argument has assumed that an unborn life is a state of affairs that is on all fours with some situation in our existence or an activity in my personal experience. In other words, what we mean by "life" in this context has not been clarified. As a result Christian judgements that would be seen as clear applications of the doctrine of creation, showing their moral implications, are found to be incoherent.

The logical analysis offered in the preceding paragraph is only a footnote to the long history of theological thinking concerning the unborn life. As is well known, early Christian thought was heavily influenced by both Aristotle and the development of Plato's thought by the Neoplatonists. The biblical background to Christian understanding of the nature of the human person was likewise mixed; for though the story of creation in Genesis would imply a monistic picture of the person, some later parts of the Old Testament[3] suggest a more dualistic picture.[4] Aristotle had regarded the foetus as unformed so that his notion of person was defined in terms of substance and existence. Even the Neoplatonic emphasis on the superior value of mental categories did not so much change as simply color this view. Thus, even as late as Boethius, "person" is defined in terms of substance—"an individual substance of a rational nature." Following Aristotle Aquinas believed that "quickening" or "ensoulment" occurred forty days after conception in the case of males and eighty days after in the case of females.[5] It is worth pointing out that St. Thomas' account of the soul is thus in no way a descriptive psychology; his concern was simply, on the basis of rather rudimentary science, to outline the *nature* of man, to give an account of the essential features that make man *animal rationalis*. Because of his dependence on the Aristotelian anthropology St. Thomas regarded abortion prior to ensoulment as a sin but abortion after ensoulment as the sin of *murder*. In ten centuries, then, little had changed from the early third century identification of the foetus as a human being, which we find in Tertullian. He says:

> For us, indeed, homicide having been forbidden once and for all, it is not lawful to destroy even that which is conceived in the womb while the life-blood is still being drawn into a human being. To deny birth is to hasten the homicide; for it makes no

3. Isa 21:9 and Wis 12:7.

4. See Barr, *The Garden of Eden and the Hope of Immortality.*

5. Aquinas, *In Sent,* IV, 31, 2.

difference whether one snatches a life that is born or demolishes a life being born. Even the one who is future is a man: everything is a fruit already in its seed.[6]

For Christian theology, then, the issue of the beginning of personal life has never been a matter irrelevant to the discussion of the unborn life. Dame Mary Warnock's account of her Committee's deliberations is very instructive as well as interesting.

> To ask, as people were prone to, "When does human life begin?" was to pose a misleading question. For it sounded like a question to which scientists could give an answer; and it was assumed by those who asked the question that if an answer was forthcoming, we would know that from that point onwards, when human life sprang into existence, the embryo was to be protected. Some members of the committee and, later, some members of parliament even begged that we might place a moratorium on research until such time as scientists could answer the question "when does life begin?" . . . But the trouble was that scientists would say, quite rightly, that human sperm and eggs were alive; human life does not begin with the embryo. Yet no one suggested that every spermatozoon and every egg discarded in the normal menstrual cycle would be protected from destruction. So the question being asked was not about human life but about valuable human life.[7]

What seems so instructive about this is the way in which the argument moves back and fore between the notion of beginning and the very different notion of the nature of human life and its ethical status. The latter, as we saw, was St. Thomas' main concern and that may help to explain why Catholic theology has viewed the empirical question as part and parcel of the more philosophical issue. Clearly, as Dame Mary points out, scientific facts alone cannot answer the question of the status of the embryo or foetus; but it does not in any way follow that information about the biological events concerned has no place in the formation of the final ethical judgment. In Dame Mary's account the notion of human life seems to give way to that of life with the result that the ambiguity of the latter drives the argument to the conclusion that, as she says, the issue is not that of human life but of *valuable* human life. Clearly, if we are trying to describe the origin of a human life then we point to fertilization;

6. Tertullian, *Apol.* 9, 8.
7. Ibid., 93–94.

but to argue that fertilization is the *time* when human life is said to begin is to rely on the simple assertion that a human person is the conjunction of an egg and a sperm from which a zygote emerges. The very fact that fertilization is no guarantee of development to birth is an obvious difficulty with this argument.

The kind of complexity that we have just been considering is in fact borne out by the history mentioned earlier. Tertullian and others were protesting against the common tendency in the ancient world to treat unborn and infant life as of little consequence.[8] The historical and cultural context needs to be noted if we are to weigh the argument properly. Yet what is most obvious and very important is that Tertullian could not resist identifying the life not yet born with the person who exists after birth—"even the one who is future is a man." In one obvious respect his assertion is a tautology since the pre-natal life has already been defined as human (something that is clearer in the original Latin, which would be literally translated as "a man is he who is future") so that the identity is guaranteed. One further point needs to be made about Dame Mary's remarks. Talk about valuable human life is far from straightforward. In his book *Valuing Life* (Princeton, 1991) John Kleinig shows that assertions about valuing life employ a complex normative vocabulary, using notions of worth, reverence, sanctity, dignity, respect, and rights. The theologian will then once more ask, "When is life a human life?" I cannot pretend to have more than a simplistic knowledge and understanding of what the scientific evidence is concerning this. It would seem that biologically speaking there is full potential for human life from the time when even cell division occurs and the chromosomal formation of the morula is complete (i.e., from about the seventh day). Already the zygote is distinct from its parents and carries within it the genetic coding of the future person. *Physiologically*, then, there is no point from now on at which it can be said that "life" begins. None of the changes that occur in the embryo's progress towards birth can constitute such a dividing line. At six weeks after conception there is a rudimentary nervous system but no nervous activity. A week or two later spinal reflexes appear and about the ninth or tenth week the first spontaneous movements are to be seen. It is thought that this kind of movement has no feeling and that behavior before eighteen weeks almost certainly involves only the lower brain, the brain stem and the spinal chord as distinct from

---

8. See Noonan Jr., *Contraception*, 86ff.

the centres of awareness. It is perhaps worth noting in passing that even if the scientific evidence were more precise we would not have been able to answer our question; for what this bald summary of that evidence shows is how elastic the concept of "life" turns out to be. And even were we to define that word strictly we would still be left with the problem posed by Tertullian's remarks, viz the identification of the *potential* with the *real*.

It is often said by philosophers that disputes about identity conditions are disputes about the nature of the thing in question. Now, if we are agreed that there is no real identity where there is no activity of the brain we *are* agreed that activity of the brain is therefore part of the nature of a person, the matter that concerned St. Thomas. It is very important to notice that we are *not* saying that the person is no more than his brain; for even when we make a distinction between a person's mind and his brain we will also distinguish between the person and the contents of his mind. In this context we need to appreciate that the doctrine of creation is something far more subtle than a first cause argument. It is full of the complex connotations of the term "God." In his *Institutio* Calvin emphasized that the term connotes the Trinity, a fact which seems somehow to have been consistently ignored by modern theology, especially in discussion with a non-theological audience. If we remind ourselves of the way in which Augustine had looked at intentional activity to understand the triune nature of God and the development of this by St. Thomas in his analysis of the nature of the divine activity then we shall see that the theologian's appeal to the doctrine of creation is rich with notions of personal relation. Created in the very image of God the human person is meant to replicate that activity of relation. To talk of relation is to be aware of the great difference between our relation to the world and our relation to others. In the *Tractatus* Wittgenstein insists on the independence of the world and on how little effect my wanting to change the world has on the world.[9] Into man's hands the reality of the world is given so that his destiny is to shape himself as he relates to his world. God's creation of man is a developing business precisely because in creating man God creates this possibility of man's own development. What I am anxious to stress is the need for seeing our lives and also the doctrine of creation in the light of evolution. If the life we know we have is this kind of development— from a suckling infant to a proud strutting youth and on to the wiser moderation of age—then we ought to see the same kind of *transforming*

---

9. Wittgenstein, *Tractatus* 6, 373ff.

development in the history of our ante-natal existence. Moreover, in that case—as in the case of our conscious dependence on the Creator—the life is a created thing. The question we are trying to answer is when life is the life of a *person* so that the prohibition of homicide, which we heard Tertullian invoke, can *properly* apply. Here it seems to me that a basic difficulty for the theologian is that he wants to resist the temptation of philosophers and doctors to *define* personality in terms of brain-function and brain-activity. For theology it is clear that as we use the term "person" of God so what constitutes personhood is to be understood by reference to that ideal manifestation of it.

If it is objected that this is a circular way of arguing then I would make two comments in reply. First, it is perfectly clear from the way in which we have been struggling to find an answer to our questions that there is no precise concept of personhood. Therefore, to argue forwards and backwards towards something that approaches clarity cannot be said to be vicious argument. Secondly, we know that we often say of something that it is a better example than something else. If we think of serious examples—beautiful, true, etc.—then we shall see that these adjectives of quality point to some ideal. Keats' "Ode to a Grecian Urn" ends with well known lines contemplating not a particular beautiful object but Beauty itself. Andrew Motion in his magisterial biography[10] points out that the original publication of the poem in the *Annals of Fine Arts* was in a context well known for promoting the Romantic notion that Greek art embodied an ideal version of Beauty. By reading these last two lines as words spoken by the Urn Motion develops the metaphysical significance of the previous stanzas and also rejects the idea that they represent Keats' last words on the relationship between art and life:

> In order to fulfil himself as a beauty-loving and truth-telling poet, Keats must remain faithful to the world of experience, and suffer the historical process which constantly threatens to extinguish his ideal, rather than opt for a world of substitutes and abstractions.[11]

The analogy with the theologian's situation is, to my mind, striking and it reinforces my understanding of the words as conveying a theological vision.

10. Andrew Motion, *Keats*, 390.

11. Ibid., 394.

I do not pretend that such a theology as I have tried to map is capable of dispelling our doubts and agonizing perplexities as we ponder the problems of unborn life in contexts such as cloning, abortion, gender-determination, and embryo-experimentation. However, I hope that what has been said will have achieved some amplification of the notion of life. An example of how paradoxical and forced arguments can be when based on some abstract notion of life is afforded by what Joseph Fletcher says on issues of reproduction:

> Laboratory reproduction is radically human compared to conception by ordinary heterosexual intercourse. It is willed, chosen, proposed, and controlled and surely these are among the traits that distinguish *Homo sapiens* from others in the animal genus, from the primates down. Coital reproduction is, therefore, less human than laboratory reproduction.[12]

Such argument makes us realize the necessity of grounding our thinking in experience. The contribution of theology is the enlargement of our understanding when we ask ourselves what life is. The simple picture presented by our usual way of talking, that human life is a biological fact in which human decision is crucial is challenged by theology inasmuch as the Christian view is that man is the paradox of a created creator. Grounded in experience it is; nevertheless, the starting point for a theological view of man is the concept of God and the divine initiative. By so doing the theologian escapes from the trap of asking where "life" means "human life." As systematician and a mere amateur in biblical studies I always delighted in pointing out to students what a *sensible* book the Bible is. There is a wealth of meaning in the metaphors used of man—"child," "son," "image of God," and so on, all of which imply that man is what he is because he is *related* to God. Let me say in passing that I am not following Calvin's definition of the image of God as that relatedness, a notion that is dangerously ambiguous, but rather his insistence that there is something implanted in or impressed on man by that creation in God's image. So too it is with great wisdom that the story of creation in Genesis pictures man as not only a created being in a particular relation to God but also as one given a relation to his species and the world. The sense of the extent of my relatedness to humanity and the world in their historicity is one reason why I find Waldo's poem "Cofio" quite haunting. He speaks of the

12. Fletcher, "Ethical Aspects of Genetic Controls," 781

forgotten things lost now in the dust of time gone by, the old forgotten things of mankind; and in conclusion he says:

> Mynych ym mrig yr hwyr, a mi yn unig,
> Daw hiraeth am eich 'nabod chwi bob un;
> A oes a'ch deil o hyd mewn cof a chalon,
> Hen bethau anghofiedig teulu dyn?

> (Often at dusk, as I stand alone,
> There comes a great longing to know each of you;
> Is there something that holds you ever in heart and mind,
> You old forgotten things of mankind?)

The whole thing is summed up in the Psalmist's wondering confession that man is the object of God's concern and also the very agent of God in his world (Ps 8). This means that the biological activity which can be regarded as human is a relation, the kind of relation that is, as Fichte teaches us, one of intersubjectivity. This is why it is necessary for the theologian to leave behind such favorite concepts as "sacredness of personality," "sanctity of life," and "immortal soul." They suggest something purely individual and are therefore empty of the social implications of the concept of relation. As an American Jesuit moral theologian put it:

> In the past we were guilty of an individual reading of the principle of totality. The task of contemporary moralists is to do justice to the social, cosmic aspects of man without falling into collectivism. Contemporary genetic possibilities force on us a realization of responsibilities beyond the individual.[13]

Once again I would want to see the relevance of the concept of evolution; but whether or not we would speculate on the evolution of what traditionally was called the soul we should certainly resist the temptation to follow blind orthodoxy and say as the Catholic Archbishops did, that what begins at conception is "the life not of a potential human being but of a human being with potential."[14] I do not want to make partisan or cheap comments on Catholic Bishops and Archbishops; *but* I think it is a great pity that they did not realize how far they lagged behind their own moral theologians. The great Bernard Häring in his book *Medical Ethics* adopts a position much like what I have tried to expound. He speaks of

13. McCormick, S.J., "Genetic Medicine," 549.

14. *Abortion and the Right to Life: A Joint Statement of the Catholic Archbishops of Great Britain*, 1980, Para. 12.

the development of the cerebral cortex as what "hominizes" man. Though he does not see this as legitimizing abortion he states bluntly that "at least before the twenty-fifth to fortieth day, the embryo cannot yet with certainty be considered a human person."[15] It is in fact not sufficiently appreciated that until fairly recently the orthodox view of the embryo was not as simplistic as the view of the Archbishops. Thus, at the end of the fourth century Gregory of Nyssa appeals to a distinction between "fully human" and "potentially human" as something he could take for granted. The context of his argument is the nature of orthodox belief but this is what he says on our matter:

> It would not be possible to style the unformed embryo a human being but only a potential one—assuming that it is completed so as to come forth to human birth, while so long as it is in this unformed state it is something other than a human being.[16]

The potential is not the actual and we confuse ourselves if we treat it as such. Careless grammar can produce the vicious logic of a quantification shift. If we recall Gray's "Elegy in a Country Churchyard" we can appreciate the error that only sentimentality elevates to proper judgement. The churchyard would doubtless be the resting-place of talent, but a mute inglorious Milton there would not therefore be found there.

It might be argued that this discussion has been metaphysical rather than moral in so far as no problem of action has been discussed. However, the moral relevance of this has been shown by R. M. Hare in his essays "Possible People" and "When Does Potentiality Count?"[17] In the first he argues that "where we have a choice between bringing someone into existence and not doing so the interests of that possible person have to be considered" and remarks that there is an "obvious relevance" to such topics as abortion and embryo experimentation.[18] Hare writes very movingly about the times when he got near wishing that he did not exist and especially about his experience as a prisoner of war in the Far East. What this experience shows, he says, is "that there is a limit below which no-existence becomes preferable."[19] Regarding duty to the possible person, his contention is that "in considering whether to bring a new

15. Häring, *Medical Ethics*, 84.

16. Gregory of Nyssa, *Adversus Macedonianos*, 320.

17. Hare, *Essays in Bioethics*, chapters 5 & 6.

18. Ibid., 67.

19. Ibid., 75.

person into existence I have to look at the question as if I were going to be that person" and that if his existence would be moderately agreeable then "I am constrained by universalibility to treat this fact as just as relevant to my moral thinking as a similar fact about my own actual existence."[20] In much the same way Hare insists that the potentiality of the embryo to develop into a grown person "is important just because, if it does, that grown person will benefit."[21] Though these arguments are weighty and would seem to go against what I have been saying they do not defeat the contention that the potentiality of the embryo to be a person is not the same as being a potential person. The child being father to the man is an entirely different kind of consideration; for here we are talking of the known actual. The biological identity between the embryo, the neonate, and the grown person is not the identity that is known by the person himself or herself. There is perhaps a real danger that we confuse ourselves by what we know of the science of human development. It is worth recalling the warning of Marjorie Greene, that our paradigm of explanation of anything real is in terms of molecules.[22] The fact that we are talking of human lives, lives that depend on our present action, makes this something of vital concern to us. Yet I cannot forget the sober warning of Coleridge when he observes in *Biographia Litteraria* that issues that are merely possible move us easily to pity which in real circumstances we do not show. And if I am challenged to come back to the question of identity I think it is most important to ask whether the concept of identity is not simply inapplicable to unactualized possibles.[23]

A somewhat different but related problem is that of "designer babies," which received public attention in 2003 because the life of a sick child could be saved only by a sibling "born to order." This moved the chairman of the UK's Human Fertilization and Embryology Authority (H.F.E.A.) to declare that Britain's fertility laws should be overhauled to tackle the ethical question of "designer babies." The law needed updating to expand the authority's remit so that patients were better protected and to consider the moral implications of a technology barely thought possible when the legislation was framed. Such revision should broaden the range of fertility treatments requiring an H.F.E.A. licence.

20. Ibid., 73.
21. Ibid., 87.
22. Marjorie Greene, *The Knower and the Known*, 185.
23. Cf. Quine, *From a Logical Point of View*, 4.

The controversy over "designer babies" and "saviour siblings" had also shown that the law needed to take account of scientific advance such as genetic diagnosis. That plea in itself, of course, makes no moral judgment but it illustrated how this is an area where the theologian as much as the legislator must keep abreast of developments. As for designer babies the crucial objection to such a practice must be that no theological evaluation of the person could admit that a child should be born for somebody else's benefit.

What can be included under the heading of embryo experimentation is research on human stem cells; and the last decade or so has seen it result in the promise of therapy for the tragic conditions of Parkinson's Disease and Alzheimer's. Cells in the very early embryo have not differentiated and so are adaptable. They are normally harvested from embryos left over from fertility treatment. Once more, then, we face the problem of the potential person; but this time we are considering the possibility of therapeutic benefit from the use of the embryo. To argue that such potentially beneficial results could not be justified because the embryo is a potential person would surely be a very strange comparison and calculation of benefit. Clearly such experimentation on embryos in early development could not justify experimentation on more developed embryos. Neither does it remove the difficulty—common to both situations—of establishing who the subject of the research is. The embryo obviously cannot give consent and equally, though the embryo can be said to have no existence apart from the woman who would bring it to term, the woman cannot give consent on behalf of the embryo. However, in January 2007 scientists announced that stem cells could be harvested easily from the amniotic fluid so that they are available from samples taken for amniocentesis. In one test researchers grew brain cells from AFS cells and implanted them into mice suffering from a degenerative brain disease. The cells successfully repopulated the damaged parts of the brain. I cannot see that such therapeutic research is anything other than the proper use of the human body consistent with what was earlier outlined as the Christian view of man as a created creator. The picture of the world in Psalm 8 as given to man to be cultivated for God must surely include what we know of and can do with biology. Furthermore, the motif of new creation in the confession of the risen Lord and its cosmic significance reinforces such a positive attitude towards life in the world.

Inevitably we are led by this discussion of embryo experimentation to consider the issue of human cloning, which was so much in the news because of unsubstantiated claims. However distant or near the prospect, it is something that raises moral hackles in both religious and secular contexts. I have offered theological justification for embryo experimentation which has a clear therapeutic aim; but in the case of cloning there would seem to be no identifiable therapeutic aim and the experimentation could not claim any justification beyond the possibility of success. If it is argued in reply that this is sufficient justification one must insist that such success is morally neutral and that theologically the justification must be the glory of God. Another—and an obvious—objection is that by creating a copy of a person we would have robbed the cloned individual of his or her individuality. It might be thought that such a situation already exists naturally in the case of identical twins; but equally obvious is the reply to this objection, that when it occurs it does so naturally so that citing this example does not defeat the original objection. Moreover, anyone who has dealt with identical twins knows very clearly that it is a situation where one is aware of dealing with two different people. A more important objection is that in the case of identical twins *we* are not seeking to determine what a life shall be but rather dealing with an extraordinary example of dealing with different persons. This suggests the Kantian objection that cloning would be to treat people as means not as ends. Stated thus baldly, it is an objection that can easily be refuted because there are many situations in which we treat people as means not ends. There is hardly any social organization in terms of health, safety, or political welfare that does not require such; but we are very clear that these are situations where the aim of the organization is the proper valuation of persons as ends in themselves. So if we see the Kantian objection as a weak statement of the golden rule then it must be admitted that the huge uncertainties of cloning make this a moral step too far. This is not something that could be described as that love of self which is the standard of my duty to others.

The very nature of experimentation might be thought to make my emphasis on therapeutic aim either too loose or too restrictive. A simple claim by the experimenter that the aim is therapeutic can hardly be deemed a sufficient justification so that the emphasis is in that way too loose. It will then be quite properly argued that the therapeutic nature of the aim is something that has to be demonstrated or else the claim is empty. On the other hand, it cannot be denied that several therapeutic advances are unintended results or by-products of experiments. Even so, there is no way in which the unforeseen possibilities can be a ground of moral justification. Hindsight is no justification and talk of what is foreseen is irrelevant to moral justification. It was surely the nature of moral justification as a corollary of humanity that led the Warnock report to make a distinction between legitimate experiments on animals and illegitimate experiments on humans. The limits of the human mark out the boundaries of moral behavior. In so arguing I am not contradicting what I said earlier about the claims that potentially the foetus is a person but rather expressing my deep-seated unease. I worry how human *we* would be if there were unrestricted experimentation on embryos. If this were the case we would simply abdicate any responsibility for what is done beyond the technical one of ensuring the experiment's success. One can hardly achieve a human good by rejecting a human value any more than in *Paradise Lost* Lucifer could avoid the fall by rejecting obedience. Theologically the virtue of obedience means a great deal more than simply obeying certain specific commandments. In the Gospel story the young man had kept all the commandments and yet is shown to lack the obedience that would give him the eternal life he sought. When we decide to intervene in our world it is necessary to remember that we too are affected.

Finally, I want to make some comments on abortion. I do not intend to offer any fundamental discussion of the problem but simply to make some comments because it is an issue that falls within my theme. In particular, as I write this, the Roman Catholic hierarchy has mounted something of a political campaign to outlaw abortion and the arguments used echo things that have been discussed earlier. The context of the campaign may well be the successful legal application made by an Irish citizen to go to England for an abortion. In 1983 an amendment to the Constitution had been passed by the Irish Parliament, making abortion illegal. What is interesting is that the wording of the amendment seemed to attribute to the unborn child the same right to life as the mother. Whether or not this was the context, in Spring 2007 the Catholic Archbishop of Glasgow, Cardinal Keith O'Brien, initiated the campaign by urging voters to boycott pro-choice politicians. He said, "We are killing—in our country—the equivalent of a classroom of kids every day. Can you imagine that? Two Dunblane massacres a day going on and on." His suggestion that Catholic M.P.s who supported abortion should not take communion was taken up by the Archbishop of Westminster, Cardinal Cormac Murphy O'Connor. He told M.P.s to educate themselves about the church's prohibition of abortion so that they could make decisions with "consistency and integrity" and suggested that Catholic M.P.s who voted the "wrong" way should be denied the Eucharist. The Catholic Archbishop of Cardiff, Peter Smith, was somewhat more judicious. He recognized that a priest was not allowed to refuse someone the sacrament unless that person had been excommunicated or had publicly rejected the church's teaching; but he thought that "they ought to remove themselves from receiving communion because it would be a cause for great scandal." I leave to one side the question whether it is morally justified for a church to seek the control of political activity so that it is in line with church teaching, which might be thought to be morality becoming a moralism. The moral issue of abortion hinges on the language used by the Irish Parliament and by Cardinal O'Brien. Is it correct to equate, as he does, abortion with "Killing . . . a classroom of kids" and massacre? Rhetoric, I suggest, has here overcome logic. We are once more seeing the confusions in moral discernment caused by the stress on the foetus or embryo as potential person. Moreover, Archbishop Smith's comments reveal all too clearly that behind the disciplinary injunction there is a confusion about the moral action involved. Despite the fact then that Catholic moral teaching allows the doctor some latitude in applying the general prohibition of a direct attack on the foetus these arguments and injunctions illustrate the way in which we allow the fact of potentiality to blind us to the subtle distinction between the potential and the actual. The problem was raised by the plea of the Royal College of Obstetricians and Gynaecologists to the Nuffield Council on Bioethics that it should think more radically about resuscitation, withdrawal of treatment decision, and active euthanasia as means of ordering the management of options available to the sickest of newborns. It pointed out that while the pregnant woman who discovers at twenty-eight weeks that the baby has a serious abnormality can have an abortion the parents of a baby born at twenty-four weeks with the same abnormality have no such option. The doctors emphasized not only the enormous social, psychological, and financial costs involved in caring for a profoundly disabled child but—perhaps more significantly—the obvious desirability of reducing the number of severely handicapped families. The moral calculus is not a simple weighing of joy and suffering. The love and spiritual benefit we can derive from a Down's syndrome child are real enough but that is only one potential benefit; and in the celebrated case of the Derby paediatrician, Leonard Arthur, it was less compelling than the actualities of psychological and social harm before him. If anyone says that the doctor should ignore the circumstances and simply apply the rule I should reply that such a practice can hardly be said to embody the respect for humanity that the rule enjoins.

I am all too conscious of the fact that this discussion does little more than reveal the complexity of the problems gathered under the title of "the problem of the unborn life." Yet I hope that there has emerged the clear and justified plea that in the discussion of these most emotive and difficult issues we should recognize the relevance of theological vision. Perhaps the greatest danger in the increasingly litigious context of medical care is that because we are now anxious to deny doctors any claim to divine omniscience and wisdom we should be claiming such for ourselves. It is precisely because theology should be inspired by a spirit of humble concern for God's creation that its contribution is invaluable.

Chapter 3

The Problem of Death

Increasingly in the twentieth century the subject of death was removed from the public domain. As Walter Benjamin said, "Dying was once a public process in the life of the individual and a most exemplary one."[1] But death has become essentially a private matter and death no longer a problem in the business of living. Perhaps this is why historians, especially French historians, were moved to make very careful studies of death and the social attitudes to and practices associated with it. One thinks of Philippe Ariès' great book *L'homme devant la mort*. It will be noted by future historians that the twentieth century brought itself to a state of great perplexity in this matter. As a period it was characterized by an excessive concern with sex and too little talk about death. There was this strong tendency to treat the topic as taboo and to shuffle off death with the best technology at our disposal. So true is this that sociologists of religion turned their attention to studying the development of quasi-religious ritual in the mass practice of cremation with its assembly-line connotations of efficient disposal of death. Some will recall, as I do, the noble sight of black horses—plumed, of course—drawing a glass carriage. I have said before that when I witness my own funeral—philosophers always perpetrate such paradoxes—that's the sight I want to see, not your common-or-garden Rolls, Cadillac, or Mercedes. However, it is with the theological significance of this—whether we talk of trends or of personal foibles—that we are concerned and we need to view this problem, as the first and indeed the next, in the light of the doctrine of creation and ask what our faith that God is our maker tells us about the meaning of death and the task of dying.

1. "The Storyteller," in Benjamin, *Illuminations*, 93.

I think that I was made aware of this in early youth on discovering amongst the small collection of books kept in the chapel vestry Jeremy Taylor's spiritual classics, *Holy Living* and *Holy Dying*. That fact perhaps suggests that Welsh spirituality like Welsh hymnody is more ecumenical than we realize. However, it was the language of the titles that impressed me so deeply—"The Rule and Exercise of Holy Living" and similarly of "Holy Dying." The point was that these beautiful devotional books reminded us by their very titles that death, like life, is a task to be fulfilled by every man.

For many years I have contended that we cannot avoid framing a theology of death as dying: indeed my Nottingham Inaugural Lecture was such a plea (see chapter 1). Characteristically one is better at saying what needs to be done than at doing the job oneself. I have pointed out that our philosophers and theologians have had much to say about the problem of what comes after death but very little about death. In my simple-minded way I think that since that comes first that is what we should consider first. We have left it to the poets to *face* death. Too often even the greatest among them shy away from it and treat us to some general homily. Thus true and significant as George Herbert's poem "Death" in his collection *The Temple* is it could be faulted on that score.

> Death, thou wast once an uncouth thing,
> Nothing but bones,
> The sad effect of sadder groans:
> The mouth was open, but thou couldst not sing
> . . .
> But since our Saviour's death did put some blood
> Into thy face
> Thou art grown fair and full of grace
> Much in request, much sought for as a good
> . . .
> Therefore we can go die as sleep, and trust
> Half that we have
> Unto an honest faithful grave,
> Making our pillows either down or dust.

There is indeed much here to ponder about the transformation of death by our Lord's dying and rising again on the third day and the nature of Christian confidence in the face of death. What is that lighted lamp that lifts the humility of a Christian's hope above the nobility of a Socrates' patient acceptance of death? But *facing* death this lovely poem is not. It does not have the rawness and starkness of experience that we find in dear Dylan's poem on the death of his father—Dylan Thomas' "Do not go gently into that good night."

> Do not go gently into that good night,
> Old age should burn and rave at close of day;
> Rage, rage against the dying of the light.
>
> Though wise men at their end know dark is right,
> Because their words had forked no lightning they
> Do not go gently into that good night,
>
> Good men, the last wave by, crying how bright
> Their frail deeds might have danced in a green bay,
> Rage, rage against the dying of the light.
>
> Wild men who caught and sang the sun in flight,
> And learn, too late, they grieved it on its way,
> Do not go gentle into that good night.
>
> Grave men, near death, who see with blinding sight
> Blind eyes could blaze like meteors and be gay,
> Rage, rage against the dying of the light.
>
> And you, my father, there on the sad height,
> Curse, bless, me now with your fierce tears, I pray.
> Do not go gentle into that good night.
> Rage, rage against the dying of the light.[2]

Tolstoy's observation seems so apt a comment—"whatever artists are thinking of, they are thinking of their own death." Rather different from Dylan but still facing death in Philip Larkin's "Aubade." It is especially significant because it addressed the problem that confronted a secular society bereft of the comfort of faith. Religion, "That moth-eaten musical brocade/Created to pretend that we never die," has been abandoned so that death is no longer naturally thought of as *janua vitae* but quite simply an end that is bewailed. Yet, says the poet, in this situation there is no sure answer—"Death is no different whined at than withstood."

Theology must do more than simply point out uncomfortable fact, more than express tranquillity like Herbert or rage like Dylan. Yet I firmly believe that there is no good theology any more than there is

2. Dylan Thomas, *Miscellany One*, 31.

good writing which does not spring from passion. Of the many aspects of Keats' work that have always impressed me one of the most telling is the sheer biographical strength of the poetry he wrote around 1820. I can never read the wonderful sonnet "When I have fears that I may cease to be" without feeling its plangent poignancy. Sometimes its last two and a half lines have been criticized as banal in their bewilderment; but, as his great biographer, Andrew Motion, points out, "their candour is their strength—the heavy-footed desolation is like a dead march—a funeral beat."[3] Similarly we cannot read "This mortal body of a thousand days"—possibly no more than a rhetorical phrase—without realizing that Keats died almost exactly a thousand days after writing it. In reading Keats' final productions I am very conscious of the agony that he must have endured, seeking as he did to fulfil the promise of his genius under the cloud of the imminent doom he had seen foreshadowed in the death of his brother Tom, whose last days he had nursed. His famous phrase "a vale of soul-making" has not only been generalized but has become so dislocated from the pain of a dearly-wrought understanding that it has become something of a cliché in theodicy, something that would have both surprised and horrified him. It was through painful feelings— agonizingly painful as they were internalized and made to refer to his own experience—that Keats thus reached a wonderfully serene philosophy of suffering. Too often is it forgotten that the young poet who thus bared his soul to his brother and dear sister-in-law had, as a young medical student in Guy's, been trying to understand the reason for suffering. Then, studying Butler's *Analogy* with his friend Bailey in Oxford, he had discovered concepts and phrases that never ceased to echo within him.

When I reread Keats I am profoundly glad that I had the good fortune to become something of a theologian. It is only when, as often, I am flippant in my replies to people that I advocate the virtue of a degree in theology as a training for that safest of jobs, being an undertaker. More often, however, I know that what I was doing was getting people to think about what it *means* to die—not the ephemeral pains, pleasures, or problems but what it means in relation to an eternal God that *I* should die. Wales' national poet, Gwyn Thomas, expresses this tension well. For instance, in his poem "Yn Niwedd Dyddiau" he considers the darkness of those fears that assail us in our final days, the darkness that is cosmic, the darkness of the dying of the light. But, he asks, in the

---

3. Motion, *Keats*, 226.

final stanza, what of the distant lights with undiminished source? They make us perceive something beyond this darkness.

> Yn niwedd dyddiau
>
> . . .
>
> Yma y mae'r tywyllwch elfennig
>
> . . . .
>
> Ond beth am y goleuadau pell
> Nad yw ffynhonnell eu gloywder ddim yn pylu,
> Beth am y disgleirdeb hwnnw
> Sy'n peri ein bod ni'n gallu amgyffred
> Rhywbeth y tu draw i dywyllwch?

> At the close of days
>
> . . .
>
> Here is that elemental dark
>
> . . .
>
> But what of those distant lights
> Whose bright source never dims,
> What of that brilliance
> Which makes us able to contact
>
> Something beyond darkness?[4]

Such poetry is the very passion of thought which theology seeks to articulate and I recall the student, recently widowed, who told me that to have started the study of theology in her very hour of grief was her release from sadness. A Christian theology of death must begin with the agony in the Garden of Gethsemane and the passion of the cross. That is the way he gave us to tread and the Christian's hope can therefore never be a grand dismissal of death. Rather it is, as Newman says, a case of "in the depth be praise." Christ's dying was no pretty thing devoid of pain, fear, and rage. So Dylan Thomas' plea for a full-blooded reaction to our death is, to my mind, absolutely right, though I hasten to say that it does not tell the whole story.

One problem for the theologian is that if we want to say that death is natural then indeed, unlike Tennyson, we say that we were made to die. That is the view taken by some existential philosophers, notably Jean-Paul Sartre who reacted against the romanticizing of death, forcing on us the question "Whose death is it anyway?"

---

4. Gwyn Thomas, Yn Niwedd Dyddiau, in *Apocalups Yfory*, 55.

His gloomy view of life finds its apogee in his estimate of death as "the triumph of the point of view of the other," the last great indignity. Here the pointlessness of existence reaches its claims—after a meaningless life "nous mourrons par-dessus le marché," we'll just die into the bargain! Now one can argue in a less gloomy fashion that death is natural and not necessarily an evil. We often describe death as the great liberator and not always in terms as fanciful and romantic as Keats' "Ode to the Nightingale,"

> Now more than ever seems it sweet to die
> To cease upon the midnight with no pain'

In "The Garden of Proserpine" Swinburne has those memorable lines

> We thank with brief thanksgiving
> Whatever gods may be
> That no man lives forever,
> That dead men rise up never;
> That even the weariest river,
> Winds somewhere safe to sea.

Walt Whitman too expresses thanks for death in his poem "When Lilacs last in the Dooryard Bloom'd":

> Come lovely and soothing death,
> Undulate round the world serenely, arriving, arriving,
> In the day, in the night, to all, to each
> Sooner or later, delicate death.
> Praise'd be the fathomless universe,
> For life and joy, and for objects and knowledge curious,
> And for love, sweet love—But praise! Praise! Praise!
> For the sure-enwinding arms of cool-enfolding death.

The understanding of death's release goes back, of course, to Plato, recording Socrates in his *Crito* as saying "When a man has reached my age he ought not to be repining at the approach of death" and in his *Phaedo* contrasting the immutable soul with the mutable body that entombs it. This Platonic vein of thought has been evident enough in Welsh funeral preaching but there has been nothing much in the way of a Welsh theology of death. Our love of music in the minor key has led to quite a tradition of poetry which could perhaps be said to exemplify the Platonic tradition. A poignant example is the work of Ben

Bowen.[5] The epitaph on the grave of this little-known poet in the Treorchy cemetery reads "Canodd ormod am Gymru a thragwyddoldeb" (He sang too much about Wales and eternity). It is a reference to the adjudication of his pryddest which had come second best in the Liverpool Eisteddfod. There he had said:

> Pa beth yw marw ond enaid cryf yn torri
> Drwy blisgyn tenau daearoldeb
>
> I chwarae edyn yn anfarwoldeb dlysni
> Awyrgylch laswen tragwyddoldeb?
>
> What is dying but the strong soul breaking
> Through the thin skin of earthliness
> To spread its wings in immortal beauty
> In eternity's ever-smiling air?[6]

It is interesting that David Bowen's nephew, Euros, has a comment on death which is a little more opaque and more reminiscent of Francis Thompson

> . . . dan wybren lwyd
> bywyd yw ystyr marwolaeth.
>
> . . . under a grey cloud
> Life is the meaning of death.[7]

Poets have been ready to remind us that death is no regrettable end but "life's high mead."

An extremely interesting argument for viewing death as, in fact, a relief rather than something necessarily evil was put forward by the late Bernard Williams in his brilliant paper "The Makropolous Case: Reflections on the Tedium of Immortality."[8] Here he considers the play by Karel Capek, made into an opera by Janacek, which tells of a woman named Elina Makropolous, alias Emilia Mony and a number of other things, on whom her father, the court physician to a sixteenth-century emperor, tried out an elixir of life. At the time of the action she is aged 342. Physically healthy, she is in a state of boredom, indifference, and cold-

---

5. See Morgan, "Plentyn y Dyfodol?"

6. David Bowen, *Cofiant a Barddoniaeth*, 98 cit. Morgan, ibid., 192.

7. Euros Bowen, "Craigle," *Elfennau*.

8. Bernard Williams, *Problems of the Self*, 82–100.

ness. Everything is joyless: "in the end it is the same," she says, "singing and silence." She refuses to take the elixir again, she dies; and the elixir, despite the protests of some older men, is destroyed. Williams' thesis is, as he says early in his paper, "EM's state suggests at least this, that death is not necessarily an evil . . . in the intimate sense that it can be a good thing not to live too long."[9] As he pithily puts it at the end of the paper, technological advance notwithstanding "as things are, it is possible to be, in contrast to EM *felix opportunitate mortis*—as it can be appropriately, mistranslated, lucky in having the chance to die."[10] Two conditions, he says, would have to be met if we could make the prospect of living forever attractive: (i) it should clearly be *me* who lives forever and (ii) "the state in which I survive should be one which, to me, looking forward will be adequately related, in the life it presents, to those aims which I now have in wanting to survive at all."[11]

It is abundantly clear that no theologian can fail to accept the first; for if an unending life is desirable it is for some reason that has to do with the *individual* life which has been created by God. That individual life is more than the body's. What the latter is can be perceived by all; but however much my inner experience is manifested by my bodily existence there remains that which is known only to me. A theologian will insist that as this is known to God so the believer can glimpse a reality beyond temporal successiveness. It is the second condition that poses problems because if we were to be strictly constrained by it then it is impossible to imagine that fulfilment of understanding which we hope eternity will bring. One thinks at once of Jesus' remarks to Peter in the Fourth Gospel—"You do not understand now what I am doing but one day you will";[12] but I think especially of David Charles' great hymn that speaks of the fullness of knowledge, understanding, and serenity, which is our hope. Williams speaks of unconditional desires and his subtle argument depends on both the impossibility of that kind of desire being maintained and even if it could be maintained it will prove an unsatisfying life of boredom. These are different considerations for all that they seem to be so close. However, my point is that both of them depend on a view of man as motivated by nothing except his finite knowledge, his natural

9. Ibid., 83.

10. Ibid., 100.

11. Ibid., 91.

12. John 13:7.

fears, and his being confined to a this-worldly destiny. If it is true that man is a creature of God's providence then that certainty, which is no natural knowledge, can lead us to accept that we know not yet what we shall become. As A. E. Taylor said, "it is deiformity not merely endless continuance which is held out to man as the prize of his calling."[13] The movement from day to day is for each of us in our comfortable life a venture of faith and how much more true is this of those prisoners of conscience who must live each day as their last and yet *must* hope because they live. I will not spend more than a moment talking of fears because there are few more powerful than that of death. What has struck me particularly in such ministering to the dying as I have done is the contrast between courageous speech and unspoken fears that from time to time demand their expression in panic. And, though I think I know what a rational decision of suicide is—exactly what Williams describes as the recognition that not to be is better than the future before one—I know too that this is less of an existence than what Jeremy Taylor called "Holy Dying." There is no need to be mournful about this. I recall one of my students in Durham, a Catholic ordinand, telling me what an "edifying death" the old Bursar in the Seminary had achieved. Calling his deputy he told him to get the dairyman in the Seminary farm to drive past in the pasture the last lot of stock he had bought. On seeing a good herd he lay back in bed and settled down to die. That was hardly an *unconditional* desire for something for *himself.*

I have referred to the significant work of the French historian Philippe Ariès who has charted the remarkable change in Western attitudes towards death since the eighteenth century. What was to previous generations a climactic moment of tragedy and anticipation is now something that is thought of as happening to others. This is the origin of cemeteries—previously churchyards now a public amenity, the park that serves the function of both recognizing and dismissing grief. This is what Ariès calls the forbidden death. At this point I find my long study of Kierkegaard so significant; for this necessity of understanding death is what he bequeathed to those philosophers who have been his beneficiaries in the existentialist tradition. Kierkegaard's stress on the personal significance of death becomes in Sartre that characteristic description of death as the triumph of the other person's point of view. In death, for him, I have significance only as someone else remembers or thinks of

13. Taylor, *Faith of a Moralist,* 236.

me. This, I think, is a mistaken use of Kierkegaard's perception that death is something that concerns *me*, for true though it is that in one sense death makes me a stranger inasmuch as I am no longer here, who I am now is something that is neither changed nor lost. It is worth hearing Kierkegaard again:

> I had better think about this, lest existence mock me, because I had become so learned and highfalutin in that I had forgotten what will happen to me as to every human being—sometime, nay what I am saying: suppose death were so treacherous as to come tomorrow! Merely this one uncertainty, when it is to be understood and held fast by an existing individual, and hence enter into every thought, precisely because . . . I make it clear to myself whether if death comes tomorrow I am beginning upon something that is worth beginning—merely this one uncertainty generates inconceivable difficulties.[14]

Perhaps the main point Kierkegaard is making here is that the language of death is self-involving. Death is *mine*, pretend as we may that it is merely something that is true of the world; that is, someone else's world not mine. Kierkegaard went on to say that one would have to be extremely absent-minded to imagine that you did not know that you were dead until you tried to get up. As something that has meaning only as I do it death is also not something *in* my world but the end of that public world. I will come back to what I can only loosely call the ethical attitude to death; but for the present all I want to emphasize is that the mystery of death is that at the moment of death I reach the one and only *final* moment of my life. Little wonder parents and others told us as children that we should not say of anything "As certain as death"; for, they used to insist, there is nothing as certain as death. In death there is for me my last decision. St. Thomas Aquinas frequently quotes the words of St. John of Damascus: "Hoc enim est hominibus mors, quod angelis casus"—"What the moment of testing was for the angels, that is what death is for men."[15] Death is an act and it is an act that completes *my* life. This is what lies at the root of the whole tradition of Catholic spirituality vis à vis death. When I quoted Sartre's estimate of death as meaningless to reject it I could have added that his view of death is that it is a pure

14. Kierkegaard, *Concluding Unscientific Postscript*, 148.

15. Aquinas, *Summa Theologiae* 1, 64, 2, cf. *De Veritate* 24, 10 sed contra 4. The quotation is from *De fide orthodoxa* II, 4.

fact which "does not appear on the foundation of our freedom."[16] It is because I reject this that I reject Sartre's depreciation of death. Precisely because he fails to understand or refuses to recognize that death is my most mysterious hour of freedom that he fails, I think, to understand the full reality of death.

I have already suggested that his profound understanding of death was one of Kierkegaard's great contributions to philosophy and theology. It was a subject that, from the very outset of his work as an author, had intrigued him—not least because he thought that, typically, it was ignored by the fashion of thought then current. He wrote as one convinced of the Christian hope. Thus in his Journal of 1837 he says, "When in the hour of death it grows dark, for a true Christian it is because the sunlight of eternal happiness shines too brightly on his eyes."[17]

Starting there, however, he went on to develop a philosophical anthropology that gave death its significance in terms of the temporal and moral nature of human existence. There was something of the Romantic about his interest in graves and their inscriptions; but the lesson he saw there was the unique recognition that an urgent *task* had been fulfilled. Death was for him a moral problem and in both *Either-Or* and the work that followed, *Fear and Trembling*, he tried to work out what kind of morality is demanded by that final challenge. The young aesthete of *Either-Or* finds that even the ethical existence that rescues him from the despair of the fruitless pursuit of pleasure is not enough as the book ends with the consideration that as against God we are always in the wrong. Abraham in *Fear and Trembling* obeys an absolute command that contravenes the moral law and by that teleological suspension of the ethical is given back the son he was about to sacrifice. So in both of these essays in fiction Kierkegaard was anxious to *show* that death is a personal achievement.

From 1847 onwards the burden of Kierkegaard's comments in his *Journal* on death is that death involves ethics and religion. In *Concluding Unscientific Postscript*, published the previous year, he had given an extensive analysis of the ways in which we talk of death. As a result he points out that if we are to understand what it means to die we must remember the difference between talking of someone going to die and all other talk of future events with its problems. Again and again he insists

16. Sartre, *Being and Nothingness*, 539.
17. Kierkegaard, *Papirer* II a 213.

that talk of death is self-involving language. I cannot speak of death as if it had nothing to do with me. Even "the lofty thinker" cannot escape the problem of saying what it means to die. Kierkegaard's analysis of the personal achievement of the self as spirit is too complex and rich to be summarized but one aspect of it can be mentioned, the "hope based on the eternal." He sees a dialectical progression from the early youthful hopes directed toward earthly expectations through disappointment and despair the hope of which is the foster-mother of the Christian life. Eternal hope is not based on calculations of "sagacity" but on God as the source of possibility. For Kierkegaard the eternal is the only appropriate object of hope, the hope that overcomes life's tribulations; and further-more it is clear from what has been said that such hope is a matter of tem-poral existence rather than a forecast of a post-mortem one. The question of immortality, he says, is one of inwardness.

So far I have spoken of issues which are, for the most part, issues of thought; but even in our thinking it has become very clear that we are thinking about decisions and that our very thinking is here close, very close, to action. However, there are very clearly issues in the problem of death that are very distinctly practical rather than theoretic. To take a step towards these let me refer to a book published several years ago by the French novelist-philosopher Christian Gombaz, *Praise of Age in a Young and Tanned World* (*Eloge de l'âge dans un monde jeune et bronzé*). It is a protest against the skewed view that one must resist ageing, that elderly people should remain young by enjoying themselves, by engaging in sport and such pursuits. This he regards as a falsification of life and he says that it is more important to find peace in accepting the fact of ageing. Quoting from *King Lear*, he concludes "Ripeness is all." Reflection on personal death and its mystery is then the background to something akin to public policy. So I turn to these matters of public policy. Even the very concept of death is such; for, ever since the advent of transplant surgery, we have been forced to search for a more precise definition of death than our day-to-day understanding of it. We have seen some of the complex philosophical and theological issues and we must remember that there are technically medical aspects such as cases of cardiac arrest sometimes illustrate. Physicians talk of "neocortical death" where there had been brain damage and though the patients experienced resumption of spontaneous respiration they "died" some months later.[18] They report

---

18. See Brierley *et al.*, "Neocortical Death after Cardiac Arrest."

that subsequent detailed pathological analysis confirmed that the "neo-cortex was dead while certain brainstem and spinal centres remained intact." It is in the light of this kind of empirical evidence that we considered the problem of when a foetus could be described as a human life. For clearly brain death in this situation is the death of the person we have known. Hurrying that situation along is quite a different matter and a bad reason for redefining death. As Paul Ramsey, the distinguished Princeton theologian, says in relation to transplants:

> If no person's death should *for this purpose* be hastened, then the definition of death should not *for this purpose* be updated; or the procedure for stating that a man has died be revised as a means of affording easier access to organs.[19]

It is, of course, hurrying the end that is often argued to be the more "merciful" practice in relation to much terminal care.

On this whole subject of what might be called meddlesome medicine one needs to have careful clarification before stating preferences. It is essential, for instance, to distinguish very carefully between euthanasia in the proper sense of the term as now used—the deliberate termination of life, the active "mercy killing"—and a wide variety of treatments that allow a patient to die rather than prolong the life artificially. One of the most impressive features of modern surgical practice is the reluctance of surgeons to intervene to make what one surgeon described to me as "a surgical assault." Thus a surgeon contemplating a palliative operation on an elderly patient will ask himself whether a procedure would give the patient a *reasonable* chance of an *appreciable* duration of *desirable* life at an *acceptable* cost of suffering. Now it is obvious that these adjectives I have emphasized are not quantifiable concepts. The surgeon cannot make a mechanical measurement; but everyone knows that there are limits and that these are concepts that are capable of intelligent and intelligible application. Thus, a surgeon explained to me the techniques preferred in the treatment of a cancer of the pancreas where theoretically and technically an operation for the removal of the cancer is possible. Notwithstanding the possibility of the procedure and the possibility of success, the difficulty and the low probability of success, however, lead surgeons to simpler and merely palliative routines.

A more usual example perhaps would be the terminal cancer patient who contracts pneumonia; a doctor who refused to treat "the

19. Ramsey, *The Patient as Person*, 103.

old people's friend" with antibiotics would be doing what is right. Thus, though the difference between action and omission is not a simple one, and certainly not one that depends on any one criterion, there is a difference. The grounds for recommending a particular practice, in so far as they are ultimately theological are not merely that life is a creation of God's but also that there are such specific injunctions by Christianity as "In so far as you did to one of these little ones ye did to me and in so far as ye did not ye did not to me." And this perhaps illustrates very clearly how Christian morality is not a legalism either in applying rules *or* in some legalistic application of Scripture. The problem of the refusal of blood transfusions by Jehovah's Witnesses who interpret the prohibition of eating blood contained in both the Old and New Testaments (e.g., Deut 12.33 and Acts 15.28–29) thus is a different kind of problem about Scripture. Yet it is an interesting example of the patient's right to refuse treatment because there has been a reluctance to press any legal action where the case involves only the patient's refusal of treatment that was said to be for his or her own good. Thus, it seems to me that even in the secular context of Law there has been a reinforcement of the theological view of death outlined earlier as the individual's free act.

Several years ago I heard Lord Raglan expound the motivations of the Bill he had introduced in the UK's House of Lords in 1969 and it was notable that he did not base his argument on the kind of considerations one often meets in such argument, that the patient should not suffer. This was all the more interesting since in the debate Lord Ailwyn spoke of

> the crying need to offer those poor creatures the one remedy one felt in one's bones that they might accept gratefully and thankfully grasp, . . . this boon, this milk of human kindness, . . . to be wafted painlessly into the life to come.[20]

The development of the hospice movement after the pattern of Dame Cecily Saunders' St. Christopher's Hospice in London has made this kind of argument almost irrelevant. As long ago as her 1973 article in the *British Medical Journal*[21] Dame Cecily was claiming that pain and suffering can almost always be controlled by painkilling drugs and other drugs. I recall that the account I heard some years ago of the Sheffield hospice bore this out and it continues to be. Even if it were true that there can be exceptional circumstances where the pain and suffering endured

20. Hansard, House of Lords vol. 300, no. 50 coll.1186f.
21. 6th January 1973, 33–31.

by the patient create a proper demand for their alleviation by active killing, the question can still be asked whether that is the only good thing to do. And if it is not then a further question must be asked—whether there is some other course of action which is preferable. It can be argued that as a human being still in some sense alive the patient has a moral claim on the doctor that he should respect this God-given life. That being so, if—as is likely—there remains the option of omitting to prolong the life then clearly that is preferable. I say that clearly it is so for two reasons. In the first place, you will have noticed that I spoke of the doctor not of you or me. Talk as we will, the decision actually to effect the mercy killing will be the doctor's and this is a moral burden that he or she will not welcome. That is why I feel that much of the advocacy of euthanasia has the hypocritical air of the clean hands that require others to be soiled. Secondly, there is the more directly theological consideration that where-as the active intervention is the arrogation to ourselves of the divine right over life, the option not to prolong life does not recognize that this life too is in God's hands. Nor is this a sentimental baptism of squeamish-ness; for the simple fact is that medical science is not capable of strict prediction and no doctor will speak of certainties—except perhaps the pathologist! I fear that we can all too easily wish on ourselves a brave new world where human life is no longer an end in itself. Some years ago there was a remarkable little piece on euthanasia in the *British Medical Journal* written by a Swedish physician. He said that he had a dream in which he was being medically examined by a team of specialists. At the end of the examination, he said, he was taken to the director who was looking at the results. "Ah, Dr. X," said he, "I really must congratulate you because I have seldom seen such excellent results. You are one of the fittest men I know." "However," he continued, "You have reached the age of such and such and as you know society has decided that people of that age should be eliminated." The memory of the German death camps is too haunting to be dismissed as an irrational fear; for it has been argued that those mass murders began with the very bold but seemingly innocuous assumption that there is such a thing as a human life, which, for some extrinsic rea-son, should not be allowed to live—the very basis of euthanasia. This argument will perhaps be dismissed as an unwarranted appeal to a slip-pery slope. Nevertheless my point remains; the prohibition against the taking of life is too closely linked with the faith in God the Creator and his suffering Son who redeems sinful existence for us to dismiss the real anxieties that are merely accentuated by the slope. The incongruity of a social policy that would recognize a fixed age for death lies precisely in the concept of human value; and whatever the strength of a non-theistic justification of such it is abundantly clear that it has an obvious basis in the argument just offered. It is therefore a concept central to a theistic morality. Very obviously, too, such practical considerations as the variability of senile decay make the policy incoherent. Nor does the appeal to social contribution as a citizen imply that someone who is said to have outlived his social contribution can no longer be regarded as a citizen. A morality based on theological premises cannot be a merely utilitarian ethic; it is not man's usefulness that makes him valuable for God and the greatest good of the greatest number cannot be made synonymous with either obedience to divine command or imitation of a love that knows no bounds.

A natural consequence of this discussion is the consideration of the different but related problems of patients in a permanent vegetative state and those which are, in Paul Ramsey's phrase, "Irretrievably inaccessible to human care."[22] Here justice as well as compassion would seem to demand the ending of that moribund condition. Cases of patients in a permanent vegetative state occasionally make newspaper headlines, particularly when doctors responsible for their care wish to discontinue life-sustaining support. Prima facie there would seem to be no justification for that: prolonging life and combating death are obvious aims of medical care so that bringing about a patient's death could not be a proper aim. However, in situations where there is no prospect of cure the timing of death as a clinical operation poses an ethical dilemma. The doctor, we would say, is bound to care for the patient, but the care is a procedure that encompasses the patient's death. For the doctor to recognize that the patient will die is in no way a medical failure. When therefore we say that for patients in a permanent vegetative state death is a blessing and a release it is not because we are calling attention to the timing but rather because we recognize that the quality of a person's life as it draws to its close is more important than the length of the period before death. In October and December 2004 Polly Toynbee wrote two fierce articles in *The Guardian*—"The Bishops Have No Right to Restrict Our Right to Die" and "She Didn't Deserve This"—and said that modern medical fashion soothed the unsuspecting into believing that the good death is "simply a matter of getting the right currently modish care," a

22. Ibid., 161.

comforting myth that is "misleading and sometimes pernicious." Her mother had died in the interval between the two articles. Hence the title of the second article: her mother had lingered "beyond what she found either dignified or bearable: it was no way to end a good life." May 2006 saw the proposal of Lord Joffe's Bill to allow assisted dying and once again Polly Toynbee expressed strong feeling in support of the Bill. She urged readers of *The Guardian* not to allow cardinals, bishops, and doctors to deny us "our last rights." She was able to quote support of 80 percent of a poll to be in favor of the right to die—even, she added, 80 percent of practising Catholics and Protestants plus 76 percent of *Church Times* (an Anglican newspaper) readers. Of an electorate of 16,000 doctors only 3,741 voted against it—and, in any case, when the end comes, it is, she said, each of us, and not the doctor, who knows best. Quoting a general fear not of death but of "the many terrible ways of dying" she bemoaned the fact that people have not paid enough attention to the good death. The right to have control over your own body and your own life is, she argued, the same principle as the right to die with dignity.

Inevitably the suggestion that people should be allowed to die evokes the kind of concern already expressed, viz that this would become a kind of general prohibition to live beyond certain limits. To this the advocates of the Bill rightly responded that persons would not be allowed to seek this assistance unless competent to make a decision about their death; but this is no simple matter. Rhetoric such as the statement that religious opposition to the proposal condemned us to waiting in God's torture chamber until his call tends to hide the very difficulty of such practicalities, which makes the problem thorny. The Royal College of Psychiatrists was not confident that all doctors would be capable of recognizing in patients the competence necessary to make a decision about their death. They were concerned that many doctors would not recognize that a person lacked the capacity to make a rational decision as a result of depression or confusion. Any proper psychiatric assessment would concern itself not only with capacity as such but also the patient's motivation in wishing to die. The result would be the elimination of the very precautions of such a proposal that in principle are meant to reject a slippery slope argument. Once again we see that the issues of life and death are not capable of resolution on the basis of appeal to obvious empirical phenomena and events. The relief of suffering and the desire to eliminate the horrors of dying are natural reactions and laudable concerns; but in the end we are always brought back to the realization that my death is as much mystery as fact.

The concept of a dignified death is extremely difficult to elucidate. While there can be no debate about dignity being something integral to humanity—the believer and non-believer would be in happy agreement—the difficulty arises when we ask how we recognize a person's dignity. The theological basis of the outlook has more than one motivation. First, it is linked with the sacramental view of the universe, which derives from the doctrine of creation. As the created world needs to be respected because it is God's work and the "theatre of his glory," so human life is part and parcel of that scheme of things. Secondly, a Christian anthropology specifies the created humanity as being in the image of God and so clearly respect is due to the person because there we see the image of God. Finally, the command of love places upon me the responsibility of cherishing a person—something stressed again and again in the teaching of Jesus. Palliative medicine is such active care inasmuch as its treatment of symptoms has no rationale other than the recognition of the dying person as a person, someone to be loved. Supporters of assisted dying may say that the appeal to the sanctity of life is no more than a mantra; but if this can be said with any credibility it reveals a failure of theology and in no way demonstrates a lack of sense in theology. The difficulty lies in the fact that talk about the sacred has disappeared from our cultural language and argument about theological issues can all too easily become abstract and ossified. We ask for evidence of God as if belief were a matter of experiment and not an issue of living and deciding what to do and how to behave. What do we mean when we say that life is sacred? Things that are sacrosanct are not ours to dispose at will; they are life's gifts, features and elements of the world and of life that we cannot own. Locke speaks of property as that with which a man mixes his labor; but in no sense is that true of my very life or the world. The wisdom of the ages is that these are not to be treated as if they were our personal possessions. The self-professed agnostic Friedrich Hayek in his last book, *The Fatal Conceit*, pointed out that human intervention in history has often been catastrophic. Those who intervened were not foolish. Why, then, and how did they produce such folly? Hayek's answer was the law of unintended consequences—the foreseen consequences are only a part of what happens. Our knowledge of the future is not like our knowledge of the past. Hayek held that the simplest way of avoiding catastrophe is to keep to a few simple rules—rules that have proved their worth by ensuring the survival of the cultures that kept them. What Kierkegaard attacked was the assumption made by the metaphysician in building his system, that he had some vantage point from which he surveyed the totality of things. In his legacy and the sombre message of Hayek I find a very salutary call to humility.

Lest it be thought that I am rejecting the notion of medical intervention totally I hasten to say that there are circumstances that justify such and that it is important to distinguish between the intervention as such and the cause of death. This is obviously the case when the patient lives for a significant period after the intervention and even when this is not so the patient will die from whatever the disease may be. The decision made by Sir Mark Potter, President of the UK's High Court's Family Division, on December 6th, 2006, illustrates this point. A woman known as J. had in August 1993 suffered a massive brain hemorrhage, went into a coma, and then into a permanent vegetative state. Since January 2004 she had been cared for round the clock in a nursing home. In September 2006 the trust launched court proceedings seeking rulings that it would be lawful to discontinue life-sustaining treatment and medical support, including nutrition and hydration, in a way that ensured she suffered the least distress and "retains the greatest dignity until such time as her life comes to an end." The Official Solicitor applied to the court for a three-day trial of the drug solpidam. Manufactured as a sleeping pill it was discovered about seven years ago by a South African G.P. to have the still unexplained effect of "waking up" patients for a short time each day. The trial went ahead in November and the trust's expert, Professor Keith Andrews of the Royal Hospital for Neuro-disability, Putney, was shown to have been justified in his opinion that the drug was unlikely to have any positive effect. Consequently the Official Solicitor supported the trust's application and Sir Mark Potter ruled that it was "lawful, as being in J's best interest, for life-sustaining treatment and medical support designed to keep her alive in her permanent vegetative state to be discontinued." What is relevant about this case is that what is deemed lawful is equally morally justifiable inasmuch as the ethic of love demands only what is in the other person's *interest*. That it was an action that would inevitably lead to the person's death did not alter the fact that it was in the person's interest. It might be said that there is no sense in which one's non-existence is in one's interest; but that is to misunderstand the situation. While it is true that generally we can see that something is in someone's interest because the person thereafter enjoys that interest it is also true that we calculate the interest *before* the action. Here we say that it is in the interest of that person that the condition of prolonged life be terminated. There is the further consideration that of any particular medical procedure it cannot be said that stopping it is self-contradictory or unthinkable. In several non-life-threatening situations it is not uncommon for the physician to discontinue a particular course of treatment. The therapy may not be achieving its expected result or the condition is one for which there is no commonly accepted therapy. Therefore the decision to stop some treatment will depend on the general moral factors of our behavior with regard to the patient.

So far we have not considered the case of the patient who wishes to die. Such was the case of Miss B. She had suffered a burst vessel in her neck in May 2001 and since then had been totally paralysed from the neck down and was kept alive only by a ventilator. Her brain was unaffected and clearly she was competent to consent to or refuse treatment. She claimed that her life was no longer worth living and wished that at a time of her choice the ventilator should be disconnected. The doctors in the hospital had refused for two reasons: in the first place that she could not be said to be competent since she wished to die without trying alternatives and, secondly, that to switch off the ventilator would be deliberately to kill the patient. In the event Miss B's claim was heard by a judge and in April 2002 Dame Butler-Sloss ruled that the patient had a right to die. The doctor's argument is easily understood; for it is surely only natural for doctors, committed as they are to saving life, to be reluctant to let a patient die. Yet it is not a well-founded ethical argument. In 1980 Pope John Paul II approved the Declaration on Euthanasia issued by the Sacred Congregation for the Doctrine of the Faith where the contrary view is clearly expressed. It asserted that there is no obligation to use "extraordinary" or "disproportionate" means to prolong life and further states that to refuse burdensome treatment "is not the equivalent of suicide." It "should be considered an acceptance of the human condition, or a wish to avoid the application of a medical procedure disproportionate to the results that can be expected, or a desire not to impose excessive expense on the family or the community." As was said earlier, it is easy and natural to assume that to consider ending a life is the very opposite of a doctor's professional ethic and the reasons are very similar to the description of a prima facie Christian obligation. One of the most important points is that we are not simply saying that because the patient wishes this then it is right. My autonomy is not the sole criterion by which I decide whether an action is right or wrong, good or bad, a Christian duty or a Christian good. To repeat what has been said before, the motivations to Christian moral behavior are more complex: they rest on a belief in God as Creator and Redeemer and the controlling story of Jesus' life which evokes the very powerful ideal of the imitation of Christ. This, however, might be thought to imply that it would be quite wrong to regard my autonomous choice of death as constituting a right. The concept of rights against God is incoherent inasmuch as there is nothing that is our good which God could conceivably withhold from us. This kind of reasoning led Brunner to say that rights have no place in the Christian ethic of Love. Nevertheless, one can see from a consideration of the case mentioned that "a right to die" could make sense because it is not against God that the right is claimed. Thus English law maintains the most uneasy of compromises—seeking to preserve and protect life while also tolerating a degree of autonomy in dying.

Turning now to the problem of one's attitude to one's own death as the indeterminate future event there are some general remarks that one must make. As an aphorism of Kierkegaard's puts it, life is understood backwards but it is lived forwards; and again, as Kierkegaard reminded us more than once, the very paradox of death is that what is for me my most crucial question is not something I can identify as part of my life-experience. One of Kierkegaard's achievements as a thinker was that he exercised imagination to *show* the different possible reactions to this. Having mapped out the three basic spheres or types of existence that he discerned as moral possibilities he also went on to describe his own Christian commitment to a life lived under the shadow of the Savior's death. Perceived thus his *Two Discourses at the Communion on Fridays* gains special significance. He was too good a Lutheran not to see the communion as related to two poles—the moral action of repentance and the religious awareness of being buried with Christ, which brings the grace of a new life in Him. Through the discourses there breathes that strong sense of Luther's that the communion is no meretricious act of mine and the conviction that something was once done which is *for me*. Luther's great emphasis on the *pro me* is indeed something that animates Kierkegaard's whole world. Well aware of the way in which death is a limit of my life so that when I die then paradoxically *I* am not, he also had seen the hollowness of so much bourgeois morality and religion to lie in their denial of death. The point of any talk of immortality is that it is mine and that it is mine because I will have died. To live, then, in time as "precious time" is the highest kind of existence, understanding the frontier dispute between life and death. This is both to appreciate the metaphysical tautology that death is this kind of paradox and the existential significance of my own view of the limited span of my time as something that is my task.

Talk of the right to die reminds us of a more general problem for our ageing society, the rights of the elderly. In the end, it must be emphasized that not only do the elderly deserve society's care but that such care is the *responsibility* of society. The responsibility is based on the very idea of society; for the moral understanding of social existence cannot be interpreted merely in terms of contract. It is worth remembering that in his *Social Contract* Rousseau saw citizenship as a differentiation of human will so that when I will as a citizen it is in support of the common good. Likewise that common good supports individual goods. Such a view of society would of itself lead one to speak of responsibility: no contractual statement is possible without its implying a responsibility to maintain and honor the contract. Yet no-one views society as party to a contract. The natural language is that of covenant from which flow the concepts of belonging and responsibility. It is worth emphasizing the way in which this responsibility is a feature of the moral identity of society. A Christian ethic will insist on this, recalling that the society of which we speak is the body of humanity created by God and that the body politic is indeed a body. If it is thought that all I have done is to slip inadvertently from moral and political language into ecclesiological language and given secular language a theological gloss I would reply with Luther that the nature of the church is community. This means that the boot is on the other foot—society as covenant is something that gains its meaning from the covenant of the Creator-Redeemer. This is the very air I breathed as a child and youth, the pure Reformed tradition that was faithful to Luther's emphasis on the unity of the church not only within itself but with the whole human race as part of God's creation.

In conclusion, I would again refer to a problem mentioned earlier, viz transplant surgery. I refer to it now not in order to discuss issues of therapy but rather to illustrate the way in which we *actually* recognize that we have obligations towards corpses as *human* bodies. Heidegger makes the very pertinent observation that even pathological anatomy (one could add, any other pathology) must regard the corpse as "more than a *lifeless* material thing." "In it," he says, "we encounter something *unalive* which has lost its life"; and he goes on to speak of a mode of respectful solitude "which the deceased commands."[23] What I am emphasizing is that the actual practice of transplant surgery reflects this respect toward the body of a deceased person by the stringent regulations governing the delivery of organs. So, corrupt and deplorable as the *trade* in organs is, yet the provision for donation of organs from dead bodies is in every way a reflection of this respect. The whole point of the Johannine narrative of the visit to the tomb is not simply that it reveals such respect but declares the message of resurrection in the very context of a tomb.

23. Heidegger, *Being and Time*, 282

Chapter 4

Life and the Meaning of Death

I must begin by thanking the Minster for the great honour done me in inviting me to give this lecture.[1] The name of F. R. Barry is still revered in Nottingham and there are still members of the University for whom the memory of his active involvement in its affairs is and always will be evergreen. It is particularly fitting for me to recall that involvement; for it is true to say that had it not been for Barry, Nottingham would probably not have had its distinguished Department of Theology. Typical of his ecumenical vision was the support he gave in the appointment of John Marsh, a Congregationalist, to be the first holder of the Chair. And before I turn to my theme let me say that I am happy to acknowledge my own debt to Barry's writings. Like many others of my generation I look back with gratitude to his great contribution to an essentially modern but thoroughly catholic theology. I think especially of his wonderful book, *The Relevance of Christianity*, in the series Library of Constructive Theology. His name joins that significant group of English theologians of the twentieth century such as Quick and Forsyth now rather sadly neglected but who will be seen as important figures when the history is written. Happily the very first of these Barry Lectures given by Archbishop Habgood was a characteristically incisive analysis of the contribution he made. There is thus no need for me artificially to make a connection between my topic and Barry's own theological endeavors. Times have changed, I know, and these days the perception of theology— particularly perhaps of episcopal contributions to theology—is that it is *de*structive rather than *con*structive.

1. The Fifth Southwell Lecture, delivered on Friday, 21st June 1991. The Southwell Lecture was established in memory of Russell Barry, Bishop of Southwell 1941–63.

Were I now concerned with the problem of characterizing the contemporary style and fashion I would be inclined to offer the term "deconstructionist" as a more correct description; for what makes it present-day is the belief that we are dealing with relativities more than any effort to negate or destroy a particular classicism. However, as I have said, I am not now discussing Barry's theology—though I am happy to acknowledge the inspiration and, like him, I am concerned with eternal issues and their constant relevance to our changing world: and it is in that spirit of a confident enquiry that I then turn to my task.

When Provost Irvine asked me to speak on this subject I accepted gladly, declaring that it had always been my ambition to give a lively lecture on death. No theologian, I believe, can be excused the task of expounding the meaning of death and no theologian can be excused if he or she makes that subject, that most humane subject, dull. I am not suggesting that the theologian is some Dr. Pangloss brought in to sentimentalize this great disturbance of our utopian dreams. Wordsworth's words always echo in my mind when tears of bereavement have run dry—"Thoughts that do often lie too deep for tears." Such indeed was his father's reaction to Samson's death in Milton's *Samson Agonistes* when he says "Nothing is here for tears." It is very difficult to find the balance between the necessity of emotional response to the fact of death, which tears speak, and, on the other hand, the perplexity of our confused answers to the articulated questions about the meaning of death. As I pondered tonight's task I read the words of a contemporary Welsh poet, Gwyn Thomas, who speaks in a volume called "*I see a river*" (*Gwelaf Afon*) of "the old mystery/of life's genius being contained in dust." The poem mourns the death of a fellow-writer, news of which had reached him near the Danube. There at a distance and in a foreign dawn the poet could do nothing but mourn; and it was in that mourning that he pondered the mystery. Meditating that mystery, he says, he sees the oldest of all rivers. Sentimentality, then, is to my mind the last thing that characterizes a proper theology of death. Rather I say with Paul—"the last enemy is death." Roger Caillois, a French historian of culture, talks of what can take the place of ancient feasts in the world of today and his conclusion is remarkable, all the more so because we have domesticated the French expression "*c'est le guerre*." "War," he says—"that's what now corresponds to the feast." In these post-Falklands and post-Gulf days these words have for a disillusioned world an all too easy credibility and indeed a disturbing resonance. However, for the moment my main concern is with

Caillois' perception that there is something that can correspond to the ancient feast and this, I believe, is life's last great battle. Talking of feasts brings me back to the present discussion—for this noble cathedral makes the occasion festive even if it is not liturgically a festal celebration. It is, then, a theological task that I undertake; but that does not mean that my concern will be uniformly religious. Rather the problem seems to me to be composed of several different issues because it arises on different levels. It is very important, I think, for theology to recognize this many-layered character of its problems: and it is equally important for laymen, whether church members or not, to appreciate that questions that arise in various contexts do ask for theological answers as well as the immediately relevant ones. So here I find myself concerned with issues of medicine and ethics and especially philosophy. Most obvious of all to me are the issues of philosophy that are involved; for death is to my mind an *essentially philosophical* subject. That it has been strangely neglected is something I never tire of saying. You may feel that this is a tiresome paradox on my part because, you will say, ever since Plato's great witness to his teacher Socrates' courageous death philosophers have been consistently describing and reformulating that classical argument for immortality. But that is exactly my point. So eager have philosophers been to talk of immortality that they have neglected to discuss what it necessarily presupposes. We must remember that this life and the life beyond the grave are not a simple continuum, not parts of the same world, not two areas of the same room or house. I recall very well the great hymn of Richard Baxter that might be thought to suggest otherwise. To serve the Lord is his share and the length of life matters only as an extension of that service. The beautiful piety and faith of Baxter find typical expression in the stanza

> Christ leads me through no darker rooms
> Than he went through before;
> He that into God's kingdom comes
> Must enter by this door.

The faith there expressed is something we can easily note as true; but we shall be completely misreading Baxter if we think that this is some simple prediction. It is precisely because it is so strong an affirmation of faith in Christ that the hymn speaks so confidently about life and death. This becomes perfectly clear in the final verse when Baxter speaks of the life in glory with the saints.

> My knowledge of that life is small;
> The eye of faith is dim;
> But 'tis enough that Christ knows all,
> And I shall be with Him.

The nature of theology as grounded in faith and an attempt to achieve an understanding of faith is what gives me confidence in this task and also makes it inescapable. Faith here confronts the fact that all of us will know. The problem then is not so much immortality as death; for there is no meaning to immortal life except in relation to death. As the philosopher Ludwig Wittgenstein says "in death my world ceases." That is language that reminds me of the young poet Keats. I have always loved his poetry but I have of late come to see the power of its philosophical insight. In his wonderful biography of Keats, Andrew Motion[2] reminds us that though Keats' original idea for *Endymion* had sounded simple enough—"to make 4000 Lines of one bare circumstance and fill them with Poetry"—his ambition was radical: "he hoped to define the immortality of the soul and thereby transcend the present." "When I have fears that I may cease to be," Keats says in his sonnet. Or again in "Ode to a Nightingale": "Now more than ever seems it rich to die/To cease upon the midnight with no pain." For him *to cease*—that's the philosophical problem of death. The philosopher Schelling says that philosophy is born of the metaphysical shock of asking, why is there something rather than nothing? How do we talk of ceasing to be? Our language is meant to cope with problems of dealing with the world we know, the world of things that are. But here at the very heart of existence we are talking of something quite different, indeed the polarity of being and non-being.

There is a further problem that, for all its philosophical associations, has about it some greater urgency of practical relevance. What does this debate about the meaning of talk about life and death matter? It is at this point that we might realize that in recent years philosophy just as much as theology has been very practical in its concerns. These days prominence is given in philosophical discussion to issues such as animal rights and the public agonies of philosophers who convince themselves into vegetarianism only to argue themselves back into their old meat-eating habit. Much more significant is the part played by philosophers in the debates about *in vitro* fertilization, embryonic research, and the dilemmas of terminal care. The very name popularly given to the UK's *Report of the*

2. Motion, *Keats*, 226.

Committee of Inquiry into Human Fertilization and Embryology, namely the Warnock Report, will perpetuate the crucial role played by Baroness Mary Warnock, the philosopher who chaired that Committee and obviously helped to shape its recommendations. As she herself remarked, she had very frequently found herself being a teacher of philosophy in this context. She never did say what the philosophy lessons were; but it is very obvious that there are several kinds of questions treated in that Report. The most pressing of them for most people will be the moral problem of research or experimentation on human embryos. Compared with this, it might be said, questions about the definition of death are merely academic. However much we refuse to think of it, we all know that in our bodily make-up there is as it were a programme of decay—Keats, the young apothecary, knew it not only as a clinical phenomenon but personally in his own awareness of imminent death—"here where youth grows pale, spectre-thin and dies." Yet that is not all that we know because we also know the puzzle, the mystery indeed, of a life's bright joy disappearing. The question remains and nags at our thought—Where does it go? For the moment we are not concerned with the metaphysics. My point is that when doctors argue whether someone in an irreversible coma has died they are also at the same time asking whether the person is alive. What may seem a single if not easy moral issue becomes a complicated problem of philosophy. We began with the moral problem of what doctors should do in these difficult cases and we end up asking the question of what it means to say that someone is alive. Nor is the problem one of finding a definition but the more difficult matter of applying definitions and criteria and even making clear what we mean when we talk of the meaning of life. Very clearly what seemed to be a debate relating to the issue of death turns out to be more than this. Life and death are polar terms—talk of the one and you talk of the other. So the discussion of the moral issue about experimentation on embryos will depend on the identification of the embryo as a living human being. The same kind of interconnection is the case when we think of the dilemmas of terminal care. The most dramatic are those where the possibility of transplanting organs is a major consideration. Some doctors have argued that a new definition of death could lead to a greater possibility of saving countless lives which at the moment are inevitably lost. Yet, as the moral theologian Paul Ramsey has said:

> If no person's death should for this purpose be hastened then
> the definition of death should not for this purpose be updated,
> or the procedures for stating that a man has died be revised as a
> means of affording easier access to organs.[3]

The whole issue of a medical definition of death, then, is a complicated one involving discussion of what it means to say that we are alive and what makes our life a personal and human one.

But it is neither as a medical ethicist nor even as a philosopher that I am primarily concerned with our topic. The ethics and the philosophy are issues with which I am engaged because as a theologian I have the commission of elaborating a view of the world, including my life and death, from the perspective of faith. What I want to deal with is the theological problem of what the Christian hope is in the face of Death's mighty power. As I meditate on the strength of death what can be my hope? I am not pretending that only the Christian person has hope or that it is absurd for a person with no Christian hope to hope when he or she knows that they must die. E.e. Cummings' phrase is an odd one—"It is funny, you will be dead one day!" To my mind it lacks the grim reality of George Herbert's words put in the mouth of Death—"Come let these arms enfold thee." The strength of Death—that's the reality. That is why I say that no view of the human future that leaves out death and man's destiny as a mortal being can suffice as a serious object of human hope. The late Raymond Williams was one of the twentieth century's great novelists as well as one of its greatest literary critics and social thinkers. In his first novel, *Border Country*, he described a son's grief for his dead father and his hope for an immortality of the dead man's struggle for social justice. What makes the novel most powerful for me is the very image—border country. The Welsh Marches, that borderland between this country, England, and the land of song becomes a metaphor for the human condition. I want to stay with this metaphor for a moment and in so doing I am not concerned with the extraordinary experiences called near-death experiences. In the novel the hero, a young university teacher, returns from London to the valleys of his childhood to see his dying father and later to his deathbed and funeral. The border country is now where he finds himself, his own inner space where he must find his own identity. That use of the metaphor is very powerful and has always caught my imagination as description of the nature of philosophical thought;

3. Ramsey, *The Patient as Person*, 103.

but even more powerful is the use of the metaphor to express the son's awareness of the dead father's presence with him. The dead man gains an immediate immortality in the life of his son—this is a border country. What I find so impressive about Raymond Williams here as always is the utter honesty of these unanswered questions about the relation between life and death, between a living person's moral effort and the moral achievement of a life that is no more. That honesty is what must characterize a proper theology of the Christian hope. The consolation of any hope that leaves out death is something so utterly abstract that it is no consolation at all. Yet if there is a consolation of a hoped for life to come then we have the other problem of saying what kind of thing the border itself is. Wherever we know borders we are able to say what the landscape is like on both sides and it must be true here that in some sense we are talking about something already known to us. So Karl Rahner, the first theologian of the twentieth century at least to treat death seriously, has said that the only future that has already begun is the life on the other side of death.

It is time to begin achieving my task and I begin with the moral dilemma of when a doctor has the right to say that a person is dead rather than alive. This is a very important dilemma because it involves not only the moral dilemma of deciding that a person has died but also the different issues of whether what is called brain death constitutes death or the existence of brain activity is what constitutes life. That can hardly be satisfactory as a definition because we would want to insist on the fundamental nature of moral consideration and the wider notion of the person as God's creature. That there is a basic difference between the embryo and the dying person has been argued by Daniel Callahan in his book *Abortion: Law, Choice and Morality*:

> with the "death" of the brain (while the rest of the body remains "alive") comes the loss of all potentiality for personhood; its physiological basis is irretrievably lost. In the instance of the zygote or early embryo, however, . . . the potentiality for personhood exists.[4]

This is indeed an important point but only serves to show how misleading a term "brain death" is. When people say that heart and lung death rather than brain death should be the meaning of "death" they are referring not to any special significance of those organs but rather to the

4 Callahan, *Abortion*, 389.

association with them of vital functions. This is why, ever since Mary Shelley invented the genre, horror stories of the Dracula variety have a certain credibility. It is the *functions* of the brain rather than the brain that Callahan values, as is clear from his talk about the potentiality for personhood. And that very concept should give us pause here; for it is precisely of persons that we are using the term death. Here as so often it is essential that we do not lose sight of the distinction between parts and wholes. As St. Thomas Aquinas said of the soul that it is not the whole of me so we must say of the brain. And if we are to speak of potentiality for personhood then it is important for us to see what being a potential person is. A human person is a complex integrated organism and this complex integration is what makes possible the social interaction which is the distinctively human characteristic. People are not persons in isolation but in society. I am not saying that it is other people's say-so that makes me alive but it is certainly potentiality for society that does. Once again we come back to this tricky notion of potentiality. I call it tricky because we are often prone to say that because something is potentially X it is a potential X. However, a moment's reflection on our experience of gardening will show us that this is a very simplistic argument. You will know of various sayings concerning the sowing of Parsley such as that it is successfully done only by a virtuous woman by moonlight. This may account for my frequent failure; but what is clear from that failure is that the Parsley seed in my packet is not potentially a herb. By contrast, we talk of those cases where early in life there are signs of what is later obvious so that, in Wordsworth's phrase, "the child is father to the man." Only if we are talking of something having the potential to be a person can we talk of life and death. I am not competent to talk about the many physiological and neurological issues involved here but there is a theological point to be made. What I am very clear about is that a theologian has a simple though difficult guiding principle in these debates. Crucial as it is for us never to treat humanity as less than an end in itself it is no part of the Christian view of a person that the dead should be treated as living human organisms. "Treat humanity as an end in itself" was in fact the maxim of the philosopher Kant and one of the ways in which he sought to clarify the nature of the moral imperative. There seems little doubt that this, together with his talk of a kingdom of ends, was the expression of his own Christian convictions. What is more to the point is that this language can refer only to the function of living the human life and the concerns of human intentions in life. To treat the dead as if they were alive is to denigrate the very function of God's gift of life. The language of the epistle to the Ephesians is very instructive here moving as it does from the physical language of a building to the personal language of presence. This is why, therefore, I would argue that the empirically identifiable latest point of emergence of mental functioning is what should be taken as the cut-off point for embryonic experimentation. I neither prejudge the technical issue of neurology nor the legal problems of aborted foetuses. All that I am saying is that a Christian view of the matter is quite ready to accept brain death and brain life as concepts for identifying death so long as the essential definitions life and death are in terms of personal function.

It might seem that I am selling a theological view of human life rather short in talking here simply of function. Just as we are naturally irritated by a question such as "What's it for?" when we look at a beautiful picture or some other artistic creation so we rightly think that God's creation of man cannot be reduced to some simple notion of a defined purpose. Even the language of the Westminster Confession, which is so specific in its description of human life as having a distinct and clearly defined purpose, does make it clear that purpose and function are something to be spoken of on various levels. It is the "chief end of man to glorify God and enjoy him for ever." So I would willingly admit that we need to talk of man as having some worth in himself and not merely for some purpose extrinsic to him. What seems to me the essential mystery of human life is that there is in everyone's life something that makes us valued by God Himself. You may remember the argument of Bishop Berkeley that the existence of anything was its being perceived and it is sometimes forgotten that he drew the obvious conclusion about what happened when none of us is around to perceive anything. This, he said, did not matter, because God always perceives His world. The same point can be made with regard to valuation because the preservation of the world, our preservation, is an expression of God's eternal and continuing valuation of man. St. Thomas Aquinas in his work *On Truth* speaks of man's sharing with the angels a natural disposition not simply to know the truth without investigation but also of what he calls first principles of action. What is of interest to us at the moment is the way in which St. Thomas sees human life as thus transcending the world and being part of eternity itself. It is surely nonsensical to speak of the host of Heaven as having any purpose. But once again I find Time tugging at my sleeve and reminding me that we are not in eternity. So, though it is crucial for any proper doctrine of man to emphasize such non-functional aspects of created life as joy of life this does not mean that the characteristic of created human life—that is, of human life as createdness—is the function given it by God as its Creator. Occasionally in the last forty or so years there has been talk of a theology of pleasure. Ever since reading Bertrand Russell's essay "In Praise of Idleness" I have thought that this kind of thinking is very important. However, I have always found that the one feature of such theology that was notably absent was any sense at all of pleasure, the joy in those innumerable features of life that do indeed, as Scripture puts it, make glad the heart of man. A theology that fails to see creation itself as an act of pleasure and love will also miss the profundity of the tragic element of life as that becomes the story of human alienation and all that this involves. So my reason for emphasizing the importance of personal function is that the Christian doctrine of man as created insists that the meaning of human life derives from its being God's agency for the spiritual transformation of the world. Once again the meaning of death is spelt out on the basis of our understanding of the meaning of life in God's world.

What has been very clear in our discussion thus far is that we cannot talk of the meaning of death as if we were discussing the significance of clouds on a distant horizon or even Mrs. Thatcher's brilliantly egotistical speeches in the United States. The latter we can be content for Mr. Heath to describe as falsehoods or whatever plainer English he may choose. They do not concern us as we are not in the Government. However, we are in the situation of life and death. Here once again the Bible is so very realistic—the Psalmist fears "the valley of the shadow of death" and "the sleep of death" and the Fourth Evangelist speaks of the believer passing from death to life. This is why of all mortal questions the question of death is, to my mind, the most perplexing and mysterious. In his first philosophical work, *Tractatus Logic-Philosophicus*, Wittgenstein wrote the now famous epigram "Death is not an event in life." It has been a remark that has haunted me and I found it interesting that the nineteenth-century thinker Kierkegaard notes the self-same insight, dismissing it as a tautology of Epicurus that "when I am, death is not and when death is, I am not."[5] As I have said already, I find it strange that so few philosophers have discussed what it means to die. Younger colleagues sometimes ask me what it's like to grow old—what it means. "Do you need less sleep?"

5 Epicurus, *Papirer* X4 A60.

they ask, "Can you work longer hours?" etc. It is a state that they antici-pate; but, as the philosopher Karl Jaspers points out, we cannot in that way anticipate death. This is something we cannot know and to have faith in knowledge at this point (and in other such "limit-situations" as he calls them) is a false faith because knowledge is extended beyond its proper limits. In life limit-situations are inescapable. This is why analogies between death and sleep are so unsatisfactory. I have known energetic souls for whom the state of being asleep was a waste of time, something that they then tolerated but of which they would happily be deprived. Being dead, however, is not like being asleep. This is what Wittgenstein was insisting on when rejecting the description of it as an event in life. I will awake from my sleep for I have been there all the time. So in fact it is the loss of life, the *non-being*, which makes death at once so dreadful and so mysterious. In Gwyn Thomas' volume of poetry that I mentioned at the start there is another telling poem, "Merfyn." The poet's father telephones him and the conversation goes something like this, "Merfyn, your friend—I saw him on the street this morning with his aunt." Graphi-cally the poet tells us how that simple name when sounded telescoped the years and a moment of youth flashed through his world.

He and I were friends
And both of us in short pants,
Boys in the stable near his house,
Cutting chaff—the hay and straw—
Turning the sharp knives of an old large wheel

(Fo a fi yn ffrindiau
Mewn trowsusau bach
Yn hogiau yn y stabal ger ei dŷ
Yn malu tjaff—y manus—
Gan droi cyllyll llym hên olwyn fawr)[6]

He asks his father about Merfyn's various relatives and gets that familiar reply, "Oh died long ago." As he reflects on the way that the passage of time has changed Merfyn and himself who once were boys and those minutes that move forward towards eternity have taken their generation and themselves he sees Time as a familiar destroyer. The poem's closing stanza goes thus:

Time's wheel with its knives is grinding.

6. Gwyn Thomas, *Gwelaf Afon*, 39.

> And what is man on the rock of his being
> Except chaff, flimsy chaff in the ancient wind?
>
> (Mae'r cyllyll ar droell amser yn malu,
> A pha beth yw dyn ar graig ei fodolaeth
> Ond mân us, mân us, yn y gwynt hen?)

Sometimes people will say that death is something that is now managed because modern palliative medicine has taken away all its fears. Not so—think of the American craze for cryonics, the attempt to defeat death by freezing the body for later resuscitation and think too of the willingness of cancer patients to endure the most uncomfortable of therapies. We would not be afraid of dying were it not that dying is the beginning of death. Death is something we would list as an evil—it is the last of a list of seven given by the philosopher R. G. Collingwood. But it is a peculiar evil—quite unlike pain and suffering. While I can say "I will die" I cannot—obviously—say "I have died" as I say "I will have a migraine if I eat too much chocolate" and "I had a migraine yesterday but today I feel right as rain." Similarly "I will die" is not a statement that is analyzable into statements about my body. This is particularly clear after our discussion of the medical dilemma of defining death. And this becomes more and more important in our discussion as we move towards the problem of a meaning given death by what lies beyond. What I am saying is that clearly part of what I mean by "I will die" is that I will suffer a bodily change because part of what I mean when I refer to myself is the body that is publicly visible. Yet here lies a subtle and important difference that existential philosophers like Sartre have made much of; the difference between the for-itself and the in-itself. I exist for myself so that my existence is not in the world for me: it is in a fundamental sense my very world. When Hamlet was asking the question "To be or not to be?" he was not asking whether he would be *something* but rather whether he would *be*. There is then a very serious difficulty about talking of death as an evil. Whose evil is it? Often we are moved to say of a friend who has died "Poor Tom" or "Poor Dick"; but as we have said more than once their death means that they are no more. Though this is true enough nothing will dispel that sorrow or its expression in that way. This is why I think that we can meaningfully speak of obligations towards corpses. We see them as marking what has been the spatial continuum of a life that was the object of our obligations. But whose is the evil and how is something an evil when there is no one there? I return once more to

Keats who seems to me to have plumbed the depths of this problem. You will recall the sonnet:

> When I have fears that I may cease to be
> Before my pen has glean'd my teeming brain,
> Before high-piled books, in charactery
> Hold like rich garners the full ripen'd grain . . .

There is no need to recite any more; for the poignancy of this—a poem posthumously published—is clear. The brief hour of his sickly life contrasted all too obviously with the length of his list of ambitions. Here too the problem's resolution because Keats—whom Leigh Hunt, Haydon, Reynolds, and others knew—is the Keats of those hopes and ambitions. He is the same Keats whom we know in his work: and it is he whom we pity.

There is one more philosophical problem about the meaning of death that once again is the problem pressed on me by the existentialist philosopher, Sartre. Death, says Sartre, is a totally "contingent fact which as such on principle escapes me and originally belongs to my facticity."[7] Death is a fact that descends upon conscious freedom to destroy it. It is a contingency that as such is not one of any freely projected and conscious possibilities but the end of those possibilities—a

> nihilation of all my possibilities. As such it is a nihilation which itself is no longer part of my possibilities. Thus death is not my possibility of no longer realizing a presence in the world but rather an always possible nihilation of my possibilities which is outside my possibilities.[8]

Though I can fear or even wish for a particular type of death I cannot, says Sartre, adopt "the project towards my death as the undetermined possibility of no longer realizing a presence in the world."[9] When death is it is the annihilation of all my possibilities and while possibilities remain open for me then death is not. It is forever "outside my possibilities and therefore I cannot wait for it; that is, I cannot thrust myself towards it as towards one of my possibilities. Death can not therefore belong to the ontological structure of the for-itself," that is the conscious self.[10] This is all

---

7. Sartre, *Being and Nothingness*, 545.
8. Ibid., 537.
9. Ibid., 540.
10. Ibid., 545.

that death is for Sartre and he steadfastly refuses any romanticization of death as he does also Heidegger's view that death is what gives me meaning. On the contrary, says Sartre, it is I who give death meaning—such meaning, that is, as you can give nihilation. My own death, in so far as I can think that concept, means the "triumph of the point of view of the other over the point of view which I am towards myself."[11] The look (*le regard*) is a very important idea in Sartre and he views it as the symbol of the fight against the hell which is others. "Mortal represents the present being which I am for the Other; dead represents the future meaning of my actual for-itself for the Other."[12] If I fix the other person with my look I make him or her an object, a dead thing; and in death I am perpetually an object for someone else. Therefore he says that the very essence of death is that it is the crowning absurdity of life—that last stupidity thrown into the bargain, as he puts it in his graphic phrase (*nous mourons par-dessus le marché*).

I have tried to expound Sartre as briefly and accurately as I can because I believe that he has much to teach us. In the first place, he makes quite clear something that the theologian will emphasize, that in regard to meaning (that is, significance) death and life are correlative. That is, it is because for Sartre life has no meaning that death too is an extra absurdity thrown into the bargain. There is no time to discuss this aspect of Sartre further; but it is a theme to which we shall return. For secondly, the absurdity of life for Sartre consists in part of the way in which social life is hell and in part of the fact that because God is impossible then man is responsible. Two things come into play here. In the first place, what Sartre calls his work is a phenomenology and there is a very important sense in which it is that—a bare account of the facts of human existence; and the theologian neglects such an account at his peril. What Sartre gives us in his philosophy and most clearly in a play like *No Exit* is an account I can accept—but would describe it as an account of fallen human nature. And in the second place, he is concerned with nothing less than nature, with reality, with ontology, and here too theology finds itself challenged. To address Sartre's view of the meaning of death is then to ask oneself whether this account of life is a proper account of its nature. Is my life a hellish exposure to others or is it the way in which I respond to a demand that reveals what ought to be? If life is indeed my look then it cannot be

11. Ibid., 540.
12. Ibid., 547.

that except in so far as I am made aware of myself by the other and aware of the other as part of the kingdom of ends. I am enough of a melancholy Celt and enough of a cynic to find echoes of Sartre's harsh philosophy in my own heart and grant that he is the best cure for sentimentalism; but I cannot escape the realization of the demands of morality on me as part of my consciousness. Here too the theologian finds matter for reflection and discussion. It is not merely Sartre's vivid use of a theological term but the more fundamental matter of a view of man's nature, of morality and society. No Christian view of man can do less than stress that man as made in the image of God is made for society, that morality belongs to the structure of the world, and that in such moral interrelations of society we understand what is meant by the kingdom of God. If the other is there from the beginning then to say that hell is others is merely to rationalize my own guilty nature. The meaning of death is never absurdity: paradoxically it sums up all life's meaning. How else can one understand the phrase in *Samson Agonistes*—"nothing is here for tears"?

If Sartre has much to teach us Heidegger has even more. When I say that death sums up all life's meaning I am far from agreeing with the view that he develops in *Being and Time*. He argues that authenticity of living entails that one clearly accepts death because the totality of man's existence (*Dasein*) can be seen only in its being-towards-death. I have already said enough about the grim harvest of time so that there is no need to pick out the obvious way in which this statement is true. We are familiar enough with Vauvenargue's advice: "Plan as if you are to live forever but work as if you are to die tomorrow." Equally the old adage "call no man happy until he is dead" reminds us of the way in which the future constantly remains for me a time of uncertainty and only in the obituary is a life's happiness finally defined. However, it is precisely this attitude of reporting or giving an account that Heidegger criticizes as our failure to treat death properly. As he says, what we must do is to grasp "the ontological meaning of dying of the person who dies, as a possibility-of-Being which belongs to his Being."[13] Heidegger's ambition, if not his achievement, in philosophy was to recover an original sense of the way things are revealed in our everyday life and that, perhaps, is especially true of his thinking about death. Reference to both one's existential understanding and also an analytical discussion is what he wanted to achieve and which, in his view, philosophy had

13. Heidegger, *Being and Time*, 283.

not sought to achieve. An existential conception of death demands that we do not simply note an absence but seek the meaning of a presence which is not empirically available. It involves indeed the difficulty of clarifying the completeness of what is recorded in the obituary but even more important is the understanding of what it is for me to understand my life as something that is directed towards that completeness.

One easily loses patience with Heidegger's convoluted argument and his ungainly use of Germanic terminology: it is often very tempting to dismiss his remarks as triviality dressed up in obscure language to seem to be profundity. This is perhaps one's first reaction on reading "When *Dasein* reaches its wholeness in death it simultaneously loses the Being of its 'there.'"[14] However, he does not simply mean to say that when someone has come to the end of their life they are not walking about any more. He wants to understand what "wholeness" means and is calling attention to the fact that, though the dead are not among the statistics of a population neither are they things that never were nor things that are no more. Even a corpse, he notes, is something to be studied with an orientation to the idea of life.[15] This was an observation that was significantly illuminated for me by a medical colleague's remark that, as a doctor, he thought his practice as a pathologist put him at an advantage over his colleagues in that he could be sure about his diagnosis. Because Heidegger regards human existence (*Dasein*) as essentially an inter-subjective affair (Being-with-others) Heidegger sees our experience of another's death as especially significant. It is an experience of death: I do not die but I know that this death is in some way an objectification of what I will know. This, surely, is the meaning of Donne's great injunction that as no man is an island I should not ask for whom the bell tolls; it tolls for me. Heidegger's distinction between the "deceased" and the dead person is shown to be a very perceptive and significant piece of phenomenology when he says that there is a world of difference between my relationship-of-being to a dead person and my concern for a problem or anything that is part of my empirical world. His phrase indeed says it all when he describes mourning and commemoration as a "tarrying alongside" the deceased. The very fact that the image is a spatial one brings home his point that when, as so often, we speak of someone's death as a loss, the loss is ours and not the loss of being which is constituted by death. So, says Heidegger,

14. Ibid., 281.
15. Ibid., 282.

"The dying of others is not something which we experience in a genuine sense": and tautology though this might seem to be it is certainly not without its profound significance.

What might be termed this individuality of death is a theme greatly emphasized by Heidegger.[16] He is at pains to distinguish the sense in which our human existence can be represented by another. That such representation is not only possible but is indeed inherent in the nature of social relations is clear: my occupation, social status, or age puts me in a class alongside others and, for certain purposes of description, I am simply a member of that class. What he is then led to say is that this representation is impossible when we speak of the end of someone's life. "No one can take the Other's dying away from him. . . . Dying is something that every *Dasein* itself must take upon itself at the time. By its very essence death is in every case mine, in so far as it 'is' at all."[17] Dying for another does not gain its significance from the abrogation of the other's death—when that will come the other will die his own death. Stressing what might seem to be obvious Heidegger thus brings out that existential significance of dying, which is indeed the reason why sacrificial death is so highly valued. For this reason too he reminds us[18] that language makes a distinction between dying and perishing: animals perish but people die.

Together with its individuality it is the way in which death is an *ending* that is of great significance to Heidegger. Death as the end of life is neither a fulfilment like the ripening of fruit nor is it a simple disappearance. It is, he says, not my life's "Being-at-an-end" but its "Being-towards-the-end."[19] A proper understanding, an existential analysis, of death as the end must, then, be based on what he sees to be the fundamental characteristic, what he calls "care"—a term that, as used by Heidegger, is devoid of every psychological and moral aspect with which we normally associate it. It is simply the structural character of my existence as "being-ahead-of-itself." "As regards its ontological possibility, dying is grounded in care."[20] Because that is so Being-towards-death is in fact something that has to do with my everyday life. That is not the same as the fact that someone dies every day and perhaps every hour of the day. It is not

16. Ibid., 283–84.
17. Ibid., 284.
18. Ibid.
19. Ibid., 289.
20. Ibid., 296.

even my saying to myself "One of these days I too will die"—because saying that, by its very illocution, distinguishes the statement from the language that would express my own dying. Heidegger has much that is illuminating and instructive to say about what he calls "everyday Being-towards-death."[21] It is something so distinct from my own anxiety in the face of death that it is a constant fleeing in the face of death. An authentic attitude to death sees death as a possibility of my being—in Heidegger's strange language, Being-towards-death is a Being towards a possibility.[22] The language may be unattractive and even off-putting but it must be admitted that Heidegger is here grappling with the difficulty of conceiving what it is for me to die, what is almost the paradox of saying that when I do that I shall not be. This is precisely what I find valuable in Heidegger. What he has been saying here differs from even the profundity of Keats' "When I have fears that I may cease to be." For all its pathos Keats' language forecasts a state of affairs but Heidegger is concerned with something general that is yet something personal and fundamental about my attitude to life. So the seriousness displayed in Heidegger's thinking has nothing to do with any morbid preoccupation with one's own inevitable death. It could never be said of Heidegger, as it could of Sylvia Plath, that he wrote himself into death.

For all my appreciation of Heidegger's treatment of death I cannot accept the conclusion that he draws from what he calls the non-relational character of death,[23] that it is death which gives my life its mineness. Sartre's clever riposte to Heidegger's insistence that no one can do my dying for me—viz that no one can do *my* plumbing for me—will not do. It is obvious that the sentence becomes a tautology when once we use absolute possessives; but what remains true is that such tautologies are full of significance. Tautologies are empty only when what makes them true is insignificant. This tautology bears unpacking. There is, first of all, the sense in which death does, as was said earlier, complete my life inasmuch as my life-struggle is now over and what I am, the personal life that is mine, is there for the world to discuss, value, or dismiss. All the evidence has been given if we see this as a courtroom or all the notes have been played if we conceive it as a symphony. The pilgrimage is now over whatever we imagine any post-mortem existence to be. Secondly, it

21. Ibid., 297–99.
22. Ibid., 305ff.
23. Ibid., 308.

could be said that even if there had been any replication of my life—that there had been two of me—when I die my life is complete. Oscar Wilde's *Portrait of Dorian Gray* is some kind of an example to illustrate this. The power of the story derives from the fact that there comes a moment when each separate life—portrait and person—becomes finally complete, no longer changing. None of this, however, seems to me to justify Heidegger's conclusion, that it is death that gives my life its meaning. How often we say of special friends and significant people "We thought of them as living forever." There is nothing incoherent about the thought of a person being immortal, though we know well enough that, as a matter of fact, nothing is more certain than death. Thus, there is a long tradition of hermeneutics that sees the Genesis story of the fall as relating not so much to the loss of innocence as the loss of immortality. Clearly St. Paul was able to *think* of a world into which sin had not entered and death by sin.[24] Likewise John Locke was able to conceive of a world where immortality had not been lost. I am not concerned here to argue for immortality but simply for the logical separability of life's end and life's meaning. To agree with Heidegger would be to deny the very logic of ethics, which for Paul was implied by this great design of salvation. The very urgency of the everyday character of the end being mine meant for Paul that an authentic existence recognized the life-giving possibilities of life in the light of Christ's resurrection.

I have moved inexorably to my directly theological discussion. First, let me once more insists on the importance of death as such; for though I respond fervently to Gabriel Marcel's declaration that "Salvation is vain unless it delivers us from death" I also want to admit that this is in and through dying. I was brought up on hymns and in one of those great funeral hymns there is a wonderful phrase about the saints in glory—they "are beyond the reach of death and pain." Yet the hymn is about the Jerusalem that we reach *through death*. What is more, it is an expression of the Christian's joy that is rooted in the death of Death; for that joy, says the hymnwriter, is given him from heaven's throne whither Christ ascended through the bloody path of his great death. At the beginning of this lecture I was anxious to dissociate theology from sentimentality and said that the theologian is no Dr. Pangloss. This, then, is the point—a theological view of life and the meaning of death recognizes that if life and the world are spoken of in terms of Father, Son, and Holy Spirit there

24. 1 Cor 15:21.

is no such thing as cheap grace or easy salvation. Life is never free and before there can be the salvation of an empty grave there is a Gethsemane and there is too a Golgotha. More than once I have asked, what is death? Who dies? The answer is here as at the beginning: it is the *person*, the whole body-and-soul person who suffers death. Nor is this language quite right because it suggests the kind of misery that Sartre describes rather than the mystery that Christian faith celebrates. We are so prone to think of death as release from our trials that the old Greek notion of the soul as the divine thing that returns to God dominates our thinking. This was exactly, you recall, how Wordsworth thought of it in his Ode, "Intimations of Immortality"

> Our birth is but a sleep and a forgetting:
> The Soul that rises with us, our life's Star,
> Hath had elsewhere its setting,
> And cometh from afar:
> . . . trailing clouds of glory do we come
>   from God who is our home:

I cannot be too hard on Wordsworth but neither can I fail to recognize a sentimentality here, a refusal to allow death and life their full value. Wordsworth does not discern the peculiar mystery that birth possesses as the beginning of a life. There simply is not that continuity from the immortal home through birth, life, and death back to immortality.

It is very instructive, then, to see how this kind of view is precisely what St. Thomas Aquinas rejects. His comment on such an apparently proper and indeed attractive expression of a Christian view of man's life is "The soul united with the body is more like God than the soul separated from the body because it possesses its nature more perfectly."[25] So in the matter of death there is perhaps the greatest need for the Christian theologian to remember that what we are dealing with is an incarnational faith. Indeed death cannot be an easy shuffling off of a mortal coil and once more St. Thomas shows great realism. Commenting on Aristotle's work *Concerning Generation and Corruption* he reminds us of the difference between dead limbs and living ones. It is not enough, he says, to say that the physical organism itself is no longer there because strictly speaking only a living, functioning hand is a hand.

But what is the meaning of death? What happens? Karl Rahner, the Jesuit theologian whose great work *On the Theology of Death* was the

25. Aquinas, *De Potentia Dei* 5, 10 ad 5.

first to bring the issue into the prominence it now holds, tells us that it is the end of our state of pilgrimage: it is the free act that ends that state. "Man must die his death in freedom; he cannot avoid the death which is imposed upon him as the work of his freedom."[26] This might be thought to be a peculiar romanticizing of death which people's histories belie. Yet if there is one thing that comes out so clearly from the testimonies of Auschwitz and the like it is this. A Bonhoeffer going to the gallows is free to comfort his fellow-prisoners and even to forgive his executioners. Indeed, if we go back to Sartre the underlying thrust of his argument about death is that he wants it to be my own free act. It is precisely because it is not for him any possibility of mine that Sartre sees it as chance nihilation. But this is why a theological account is so significant because what I am doing is going back to that secret agony in Gethsemane and seeing what that paradigm of death says. St. John's Gospel once again puts the point so clearly. As that master exegete of John, C. H. Dodd, says, the development of the picture of the Good Shepherd is very significant:

> In the imagery of the discourse the heroic shepherd goes out to meet the wolf, and lays down his life in defence of his flock. This provides the evangelist with the clearest and most explicit state-ment he has yet permitted himself upon the Passion of Christ as a voluntary and vicarious self-sacrifice.[27]

I am not concerned with the vicarious nature of Christ's death but simply with the point that if the way to think theologically is to return to that revelation and use that paradigm then death is indeed the final act of freedom. It is important to grasp clearly what we are saying. It is not that death must be high drama; for most often it is not. The point is rather that agonized or easy, quiet or dramatic it is still *my* act, freely achieved. In his last years Kant wrote a strange essay, *The End of All Things,* and he began by saying that there seemed to be only one analogy for this and that was the death of the individual. In the language of the devout, he says, this is usually called a transition out of time into eternity; and in that there is something horrible and at the same time inviting. This is why man is forever turning his terrified gaze on it again and again. What is spoken of as a fulfilment seems a destruction. As a philosopher Kant was remark-able because he was scrupulous in his honest endeavor to speak only of what could be known. So he makes no pretence to know what fulfilment

---

26. Rahner, *On the Theology of Death,* 77.
27. Dodd, *The Fourth Gospel,* 360.

underlies this destruction. To come back to my point, the freedom that I finally express in death is not something that can be reported in the newspaper.

My final point is about salvation, which is the meaning of death. I quoted Marcel earlier that nothing is salvation if it does not deliver me from death—and that is not the death of the body of sin but simply plain death. I also said that a theological account of death is given in the light of Christ's work. Now I want to bring the two things together because I want to say something about the consolation of faith that enables us to *celebrate* death. Though the fashion of Thanksgiving Services rather than Memorial Services might well be said to reflect the way death has been a taboo it is not without justification because in any death we are called upon to celebrate the mercy and faithfulness of God. I find it very difficult to think of what is beyond death and I am reluctant in my enthusiasm about speculation on this matter. There are philosophers and theologians who feel confident in their discussion of such issues whether our life after death is some kind of dream-existence. I am not one of them because it seems to me that the most important thing for the theologian with his incarnational perspective is that there is a sense in which the frontier of death *has* been overcome. That frontier I described as the line between time and eternity; but what Christ's incarnation *means* and his resurrection *showed* is that from the side of eternity that frontier was overcome. Lest it might be thought that I am evading the issue I will address the problem of what is beyond death. My revered teacher, Paul Tillich, cautioned that one should speak of "immortality" only if superstitious connotations can be avoided.[28] So I have steadfastly in this discussion insisted that we cannot think of a life beyond death as a mere continuation. "Teach me to fear the grave as little as my bed" is indeed what one prays; but that is not because they are the same thing. Rather it is like those reassurances the dentist gives you—"It's only a little prick," "It won't hurt," and so on. We know it will but we are glad to have the pain brought to its lowest common denominator. Death signifies the end of the whole person—this again I have said in more than one context of this discussion. To think of the person continuing in heaven is to pretend that there is no such finality. What am I saying then? That there is really no life beyond death? Not at all. What I want is that we should recognize the error of thinking that we can know that life before we live it. We don't

28. Tillich, *Systematic Theology*, vol. 3, 439.

know *this* one that way and so why should we *that* one? Again, that is not to say that we do not have any idea what it is. For clearly it is a life out of time and we can begin to grasp what it is by insisting that eternal life is not a life of unending time. One of the problems that philosophers have consistently attacked in the discussion of immortality is how the *identity* of the person is ensured in any such notion. The immortality I want is *mine* and not anybody else's—not even God's. To be lost in the sea of divine being does not seem to me a proper end of what God has created in me. Surely what has been created is something of eternal significance so that in that strict sense it has nothing to do with time. The task of the existing individual is to be *infinitely* related to the infinite in finite time. As indeed the Fourth Gospel puts it, *this* is eternal life—that we should know God. The difficulty is that we want to *picture* this life when we can only *think* it. There used to be much talk of demythologizing in theology and the assumption was wrongly made that only in the Bible was mythology an issue. My point is that we need to demythologize our ideas of life beyond death. The essential point is that it is a life of knowing God in which my continuity is guaranteed by his having created in my life and from my dying that unique knowledge of him that is mine. It is because we are talking of a transition from time to eternity, a change from the glory of having seen his revelation and living by that revelation to the glory of seeing him face to face that we must speak of a resurrection.

Very well, you might say, this doesn't really tell us very much even of the bare mechanics as it were. What is that life like, though? Once again all that I can do is to go back to Scripture and to note that in the celebration of the Last Supper it is suggested that this is a model of what it's like. I am a great lover of parties and when Jesus says "I shall not drink of the fruit of the vine until I drink it new in my Father's kingdom" that's a condition and an expectation that I can make my own. Nor is it a trivialization of either the Last Supper or the agony that followed to say this: rather, once more we consider the meaning of death on the paradigm of that death of deaths. Without becoming embroiled in any discussion of the nature of the wine in the Last Supper we can agree with the Latin phrase *in vino veritas*—there is truth in wine. Philosophers such as Plato have seen the Banquet as a model of life in Truth and doubtless there are many reasons for doing so. I want to mention briefly only two points that are powerful motifs in Plato's philosophy and theology. Such consideration, I imagine, would have been very much in the minds of the patristic theologians who venerated Plato as an anticipation of Christian truth.

The first is that there can be no banquet without a sharing. In his theory of knowledge just as much as in his political theory Plato was concerned to understand what *sharing* means—how the weaker glories of earthly shadows share in the effulgence of eternity. The mystery of this, which fascinated the mathematician in him as much as the mystic, was how there was a sharing that did not bring the business to an end, the mystery of Moses' burning bush, if you like. The life in Truth is a social existence of that kind. Secondly—and related to this—there can be no sharing unless there are individual agents to do the sharing. As I have said earlier, it is important for us that our death does not lead to some existence that annihilated our individuality. What is at issue here is not whether God can or cannot transform our earthly body, as St. Paul says, but rather whether he can properly be conceived to offer individual man an existence that is other than individual. Theology has always been concerned to emphasize the consistency of divine activity and just as some medieval theologians were anxious to deny that God could be conceived as destroying anything he created so I am insisting that what he creates in individual human life is what a human life must be. So when I say that it is to a party that the agony of death leads I am indeed describing the life beyond the grave as something that is as morally valuable as it is concretely real. This is the kind of meaning we seek in death as in life; and that is a fundamental matter. As Victor Frankl says,

> Man's search for meaning is a primary form of his life and not a secondary "rationalisation" of instinctual drives. This meaning is unique and specific in that it must and can be fulfilled by him alone: only then does it achieve a significance that will satisfy his own will to meaning.[29]

I began by speaking of life's mystery and I end by pointing to the mystery of life's providence that the grave is not the end of life. As man gazes at the dark sky of loss he perceives the stars of life eternal which is his hope. Again Keats puts the matter so compactly and powerfully:

> How strange it is that man on earth should roam,
> And lead a life of woe, but not forsake
> His rugged path; nor dare he view alone
> His future doom which is but to awake.

---

29. Frankl, *Man's Search for Meaning*, 154.

Chapter 5

Life, Death, and Paradise
The Theology of the Funeral

Though death is clearly the focus of the funeral, the funeral—to state the obvious—is something performed by the living for the dead. Also a funeral shows how death is related to various issues of life in this world and notions about time and reality that are theologically inter-related. A funeral celebrates a life and so involves the notion of the meaning of life—any life and not just that particular life celebrated. The minister proclaims the message of life's meaning, which is a word of hope at a time of despair and a word of comfort to those who mourn. In the funeral too the deceased passes into history and out of the context of our daily business so that at the very heart of the funeral service there is the theological issue of the status of the person remembered and in some way commended. Finally, in the message to the bereaved there is the proposal of a policy of behavior as well as that metaphysical statement just mentioned: as the Psalmist puts it, we are encouraged to "number our days and apply our hearts to wisdom" (Ps 90:12). This, then, is how I want to consider the theology of the funeral. I speak of the *theology* of the funeral because it seems to me that the minister's message here is no different from his normal message. A sermon, in Bishop Stubbs' famous phrase is "about God and about twenty minutes"; and a vital part of preaching must be the Christian message about death. If death has become something about which we no longer speak it is all the more important that the minister should again and again expound the message of hope to his regular congregation.

For the most part, in our society we shuffle by death. The process of the funeral service is something that in my own lifetime has become much neater and more efficient. An unfortunate consequence of this is that all too often the funeral service is anonymous. Rarely do the bereaved protest against this. They are more likely to thank the parson for "a nice funeral service." All too often death is for many both comfortless and without fear, a non-event. Besides the psychological effects of such an ignoring of death there is the more important *ethical* consequence that we neither properly value the life that has ended nor apply ourselves to that—perhaps secondary but still urgent—task of bringing our hearts to wisdom. It is a public duty that is particularly important if one is in the position of having made promises to the deceased about the funeral. I do not think that there is anything peculiarly Welsh in the notion of a respectable funeral, though I hasten to say that the Welsh expression of that concept—*angladd parchus*—has infinitely more meaning than the legal requirement of a seemly despatch. Talking of obligation to those who are dead inevitably reminds us of the classic instance of Crito who performed the last office for Socrates. In answer to Socrates' statement "I owe a cock to Asclepius" he had answered "It shall be done."[1] That the fulfilment of the promise in this context was a sacramental act makes it a particularly relevant example in our context as many, if not indeed most of our obligations to the dead are so connected. John McCrae's poem "In Flanders Field" speaks of the kind of obligation that those who have died lay upon those who survive. No general rule can be formulated to make such bidding to keep faith a command. In general it is clear that it is better to keep a promise than to break it; but that is not the same as saying that we *ought* to do so. If it is not, the normal way in which we might justify such a neutral action would be a form of act-utilitarianism, pointing out the social benefits of the results of the action. However, the difficulty is that it is impossible to say what actually results from my simple action of keeping a promise. What is, of course, of special significance is that the person who dies will not in fact witness any such results. Discussing the nature of promises that are not known to others J. D. Mabbott argued that on the basis of act-utilitarianism such could be broken without any detriment to the general principle that a promise should be kept.[2]

One reaction to this kind of argument would be that it does not meet the particular difficulty of *my* keeping a promise made to my friend now dead. In other words, it is not a matter of saying that a contract

1. Plato, *Phaedo*, 11 F.
2. Mabbott, "Punishment," 155–57.

made is no longer valid because one party is no longer a public agent. Nor is it a matter of one party being no longer able to benefit from the contract making the contract ineffectual. Rather what matters is my own behavior. We recall Polonius' courtly advice to his son—"This above all: to thine own self be true." His argument was that if such a course of action were followed then no kind of dishonor would besmirch his name—"And it must follow, as the night the day, Thou canst not then be false to any man."[3] Such a fidelity to what Freud might have termed one's ego-ideal would demand that when making the promise that locution was seen as self-involving. Of anyone who does not keep his promise the first thing one is likely to say is that he did not mean to keep it—that is, the speech-act was an insincere one. It is clear that sincerity is a more general matter of moral behavior than promising; and in that case is not dependent on any logical analysis of the action of promise but more likely to be presupposed by it. It would also follow, I think, that the principle that one ought to keep one's promise is not invalidated by the death of the person to whom the promise was made. I have used the term fidelity, which is precisely the notion that Gabriel Marcel employs to describe what he calls a true and stable relation between the living and the dead. From his earliest thinking Marcel has spoken of the presence of the dead: it is something that makes promises made to the now dead person in every relevant way like a promise to the living. It is a cliché that the subject of death is loaded with taboo; but, like many clichés, it is strangely illuminating. It illumines our embarrassment, which has something to do with metaphysics, ethics, and theology. I have referred to the way in which in my own lifetime I have seen changes and this is one. Taboo there always was in abundance in my childhood experience of death—the tiptoe approach to the house of the dead or the dying, the almost macabre interest in the coffin-cart, the funeral bier, or the funeral carriage with its magnificent black horses. Part of that taboo was the *respect* that, as far as I can recall, was not something I was ever taught. It was so much part of my way of life that to this day I cannot witness a funeral procession without showing respect. In contemporary reactions to an impending funeral I see something of a polarization of attitudes. On the one hand, there is the extreme logical development of the quest for efficiency in those guides to a D.I.Y. funeral, reminding us that neither a parson nor even an undertaker is legally required. On the other, there is the

---

3. Shakespeare, *Hamlet*, Act 1 Scene III, 77–79.

very different aesthetic development witnessed by the popularity of the revival of funeral *processions*—and of horse-drawn carriages. This changed thought-world is the kind of phenomenon that has been discussed by more than one author in recent years. There is the classic work by the French historian Philip Aries, *L'homme devant la mort*, the English title of which would describe it simply as a history of "Western attitudes toward death from the Middle Ages to the present." Parallel to that great work is that of W. A. de Peter, *Immortality: Its History in the West*. One could continue with a long list to the most recent, Tony Walter's *The Eclipse of Eternity: A Sociology of the Afterlife*. Of greater relevance to this discussion is the more modest work of Frederick Hoffman, *The Mortal No: Death and the Modern Imagination*. Though it describes itself as an effort in "the history of man's attempts to account for violence, to anticipate it and to adjust to its dislocations" it is in fact a rhetoric of death in a post-liberal ideology. It is indeed an account of Western literature from Stendahl to Sartre. The rhetoric is afforded by the organization of this literature around three themes—grace, violence, and self. Professor Hoffman traces in some detail the secularization of grace, relating this to what he regards as a normal but largely lost connection between life and death—that the inevitable event of death is something for which we can prepare in life. I leave aside his argument about the relation of violence to this and pick up his thesis. Deprived of a normal connection with death but faced with the inevitability of his own dying, the modern man as revealed in this literature seeks new definitions of the self-in-process, in a unique self-consciousness and in values derived from these two. This logical analysis of the history seems to me wrong. What our cultural history shows is a different thought-movement, viz the prior advent of these new kinds of self-definition and the waking appreciation of the consequences of such. To describe this as our *history* is to seek to escape our responsibility for these views and beliefs. Man himself is responsible for understanding what it means to die.

There are many interesting philosophical problems involved in understanding the meaning of death but I turn at once to the theological issues. I begin with the traditional doctrine that Milton encapsulated in the opening lines of *Paradise Lost* with his reference to "man's disobedience and the fruit of that forbidden tree whose mortal taste brought death into our world." Death is thus regarded as the consequence of and the punishment for the original sin of Adam in the Garden of Eden. Without entering into any detailed exegetic or hermeneutical discussion it can be said that it is by no means obvious that the story of Eden is con-cerned with the origin of sin.[4] The late James Barr emphatically rejected such an interpretation, arguing that the story is rather one of how human immortality was almost gained but in fact lost.[5] The familiar inter-pretation of the story as an account of the fall of man was in his view essentially the work of St. Paul who in Romans chapter 5 verse 12 makes sin the consequence of one man's fall and death the result of sin. That analogical argument of Romans 5, the Adam typology, is again, for Barr, "very much Paul's own property," and there is, in his opinion, only a nar-row basis for it within the New Testament. Neither is it legitimate, he says, to argue that though Adam and Eve did not die they were *condemned* to death.[6] According to Barr, the absence of guilt and tragedy from the story makes it very doubtful whether the story sought to correlate death with the origin of sin. Genesis chapter 1 is indeed silent on the creation of death but it would appear from texts such as Deuteronomy 32:39 and Psalm 54:29 that death is a feature of creation itself. Barr concludes this argument by saying "that for much of the Hebrew Bible death, so long as it was in proper time or in good circumstances, was both natural and proper in God's eyes."[7] It is not the issue of interpreting the Genesis story correctly that concerns me here but simply the importance of reading it critically. If we do so then it becomes clear that the fall of Adam as the origin of sin is itself a complicated issue in biblical theology and making it the explanation of death as a feature of human existence may well have little or no justification. In this complicated issue of original sin and the fall of Adam the question that concerns us is the relatively simple issue whether this doctrine is a proper explanation of death. It is interesting to see that John Locke in his *Reasonableness of Christianity* rejects original sin and argues that Christ redeems mankind not from original sin but from the loss of immortality, which was the consequence of the fall. By the fall Adam "lost paradise, wherein was tranquillity and the tree of life, i.e. lost bliss and immortality. . . . Death then entered, shewed his face

---

4. Note: The literature on the issue, though perhaps not immense, is certainly forbidding—ranging from the elegant F. R. Tennant's *The Origin and Propagation of Sin*, 1903, through the great work of M. P. Williams, *The Idea of the Fall and Original Sin*, 1927, to G. Vandervelde, *Original Sin: Two Major Trends in Contemporary Roman Catholic Reinterpretation*, 1975.

5. Barr, *The Garden of Eden and the Hope of Immortality*, 4.

6. Ibid., 10.

7. Ibid., 56.

which before was shut out and not known."[8] For Locke it was perfectly clear that there is no sense in which sin can be culpable if it is not one's own—"everyone's sin is charged upon himself alone."[9] Not surprisingly Locke is given a chapter to himself in a book by Richard K. Fenn.[10] Fenn is more concerned with *Some Thoughts concerning Education* than with *The Reasonableness of Christianity* but he emphasizes that for Locke penitence becomes *the* way of life for the Christian soul. To return to our theme, as Adam was ejected from paradise so for Locke all his posterity were born out of it. However, that is no punishment of the seed of Adam for Adam's sin—unless, says Locke, we call "keeping one from what he has no right" a punishment and that is nonsense.[11] Mortal life is still God's gift to men—"they could not claim it as their right, nor does he injure them when he takes it from them."[12] Thinking of the history of mankind in any other way is, for Locke, "foolish metaphysics" so that "though all die in Adam, yet none are truly punished, but for their own deeds."[13] From this estate of death Christ restores all men to life. This life "is that life which they receive again at the Resurrection."[14]

Locke complicates the issue in a fashion that is perhaps typically Puritan when he insists that death is the just desserts of all men as sinners—"an exclusion from paradise and the loss of immortality is the portion of sinners."[15] Since all have sinned it follows that no one could have eternal life and bliss. That would be the case "if God had not found a way to justify some, i.e. so many as obeyed . . . the law of faith."[16] From this it is clear that Locke had considerable difficulty in sorting out the various issues that are involved in talking of death and sin. While he was anxious to remove any suggestion of necessity or biological heritage from our understanding of sin he was not prepared to abandon the understanding of death as a penalty for sin. What he does in fact is something that characterizes much Protestant theology in succeeding generations—he

8. Locke, *The Reasonableness of Christianity*, 26.

9. Ibid., 9.

10. Fenn, *The Persistence of Purgatory*, chapter 4.

11. Ibid.

12. Ibid.

13. Ibid.

14. Ibid., 29.

15. Ibid.

16. Ibid.

asserts that the generality of the connection has to do with the universality of sin. It is indeed interesting that thus he shows a characteristic reticence in defining the nature of Adam's legacy—*how*, that is, it is that what happened to Adam is a perpetual historical situation: but the most significant point is that he reinforces the view of death as the punishment for sin.

What we have been considering is the traditional view in both Protestant and Catholic theology. Of the former I mention but two examples. In his highly influential *Outlines of Theology* A. A. Hodge says, "The entire penalty of the law including all the spiritual, physical, and eternal penal consequences of sin is called death in Scripture."[17] For E. A. Litton death "is the consequence of that primal prevarication by which man fell."[18] The Catholic position likewise is that death is a consequence of original sin.[19] Having made clear in his classic essay, *The Theology of Death*, that he dissociates the possibility of death from Adam's sin, Karl Rahner has further clarified the complexity of the Scriptural basis to our theology of death in *Foundations of Christian Faith*.

> The biblical story about the sin of the first person or first persons in no way has to be understood as an historical, eyewitness report. The portrayal of the sin of the first man is rather an aetiological inference from the experience of man's existential situation in the history of salvation to what must have happened "at the beginning" if the present situation of freedom actually is the way it is experienced and if is accepted as it is.[20]

With this comment we can begin to review the traditional doctrine; for his first sentence very gently points to the fundamental flaw. A critical understanding of Genesis will not allow us to regard it as historical evidence *of any kind*. Since that is the case then no statement of a causal connection between the paradise story and the recorded history of man as mortal is possible. What is possible is indeed only the kind of thing that he goes on to mention, some strange kind of inference which is in fact the converse of the traditional doctrine's hermeneutic.

17. Hodge, *Outlines of Theology*, 548.

18. Litton, *Introduction to Theology*, 545.

19. See Denzinger, *Enchiridion Symbolorum, Definitionum et Declarationum de Rebus Fidei et Morum*, 31st ed., 1957, 101, 109a, 175, 788f.; Denzinger and Metzer, *Enchiridion Symbolorum, Definitionum et Declarationum de Rebus Fidei et Morum*, 33rd ed., 1965, 413.

20. Rahner, *Foundations of Christian Faith*, 114.

Understanding Scripture critically does furthermore enable us to see something more profound in the story. For the point of there being a tree of the knowledge of good and evil in the garden is that thus the story shows the reality of man's capability of refusing the creation. Man can refuse the gift given by God. Man is placed in the garden; that is, in the area of God's first decision. But no animal he, he is called upon, of his own free will, to ratify God's decision. Luther's comment on this chapter of Genesis is very profound. He refers to the tree as a temple and points out that Satan tempts Adam not to kill, to fornicate, or do anything such. That "first sin" is not such and such an *act* but a fundamental *attitude* towards God. Regarding the traditional doctrine, then, I would want to emphasize two points. In the first place, the mythological nature of the Genesis story demands a reading very different from the naïve assumption that it is because Adam fell that the biological condition and existential situation of man is that of mortality. I should stress that this is more than a simple rejection of the historicizing of the myth as a pre-history of the human race. Quite apart from this false reading of Scripture as a quasi-science the traditional doctrine is a false reading of Scripture even as myth; for it is *broken relationship* rather than crime and punishment that is its theme.

Tillich's comments on the story show very well how the story is concerned with the nature of sin rather than its causal effects. He says:

> It is the profoundest and richest expression of man's awareness of his existential estrangement and provides the scheme in which the transition from essence to existence can be treated. It points, first, to the possibility of the Fall; second, to its motives; third, to the event itself; and fourth, to its consequences.[21]

There is no need to follow the account in detail; but it is instructive to note that Tillich finds the very possibility of the fall to be the distinguishing mark of man that enables him to serve the divine glory.[22] As for the "event" itself he sees it arising from the anxiety that is man's state as the awareness of his finitude. Man's finite freedom makes possible the transition from essence to existence and his decision to reject the dreaming innocence of his essential being and to opt for self-actualization.[23] This transition from essence to existence is a "universal quality of finite

21. Tillich, *Systematic Theology*, vol. 2, 35.
22. Ibid., 37.
23. Ibid., 41.

being."[24] This account, which is avowedly mythological, is what Tillich offers as his doctrine of man's nature and situation. Creation and fall coincide, he says; and there never was a time when created goodness was actualized—there never was a utopian paradise.[25] While I would not follow Tillich's analysis in every respect his sensitive interpretation of the Genesis myth does clarify my point. It is not to some first sin that we look for the cause of mortality any more than for the cause of sin's universality. Consequently, my first point is that in the traditional theology of death we have not in fact been given the causal explanation it is assumed to provide.

The second point is perhaps the other side of the first, viz that the original sinfulness of man is an important feature of the theology of death. What I mean is this—any theological account of death must do more than simply note the philosophical error of talking in terms of a causal origin. Theology notes that, as a situation in man's relation with God, death like life finds man in sin. To quote Rahner once more, "original sin expresses nothing else but the historical origin of the present, universal and ineradicable situation as co-determined by guilt."[26] What this means is that the connection between sin and death is *accidental*. This important point was what Reinhold Niebuhr expressed in his famous paradox that sin is inevitable but not necessary. The whole tragedy of man is not that he should die but rather that he has mixed up with death's inevitability something that is not necessary, viz sin. Tillich's interpretation of original sin is a brave attempt to spell out that paradox by showing the close relation between man's development of individuality and the process of alienation, which is the essential nature of sin. Though Tillich sometimes blurs the distinction between the activity or action of sin, on the one hand, and its cause, on the other, he is surely right when he says that the truth of the doctrine of original sin is that sin is fact before it is act.

What I have argued so far is that man's mortality is wrongly conceived if we see it as in any sense a consequence of his sinful history. Mortality, I contend, is no accident of his creation but a necessary feature of it. That seems to me to be implied by the very finitude of the world that is created and of which man is a part. It is very interesting that Barth—for whom, as is very obvious from his *Dogmatics*, theology involves a real

24. Ibid., 42.
25. Ibid., 50.
26. Ibid.,114.

devotion to the exposition of Scripture—views the Genesis narrative as a picture of the created world as something finite. It is specific, limited, given a *human* definition and is there as and for a covenantal relation between God and man. All this must mean that to treat the story of Eden as immortal man's paradise is quite wrong, despite the way in which this interpretation unites such strange bed-fellows as Locke and A. A. Hodge. As I have tried to make clear, making Eden some kind of historical explanation of man's condition is futile precisely because it *explains* nothing. In his great essay *On the Theology of Death* one of Rahner's crucial points was that even if man had not sinned God would still have brought his life to a temporal end. This will seem less obscure if we consider what Tillich has to say about time as a category of existence. In his first volume of *Systematic Theology* Tillich gives the finest categorial analysis in all twentieth-century theology and possibly the most impressive such metaphysical effort since Kant's *Critique of Pure Reason*. "The categories," he says, "are forms of finitude."[27]

Tillich's analysis of time is profoundly helpful because he stresses the ambiguity of time. After pointing out the positive element in time he continues:

> On the other hand, it is impossible to overlook the fact that time "swallows" what it has created, that the new becomes old and vanishes, and that creative evolution is accompanied in every moment by destructive disintegration. . . . The melancholy awareness of the trend of being toward non-being, a theme which fills the literature of all nations, is most actual in the anticipation of one's own death. What is significant here is not the fear of death, that is the moment of dying. It is anxiety about *having* to die which reveals the ontological character of time.[28]

Time is the central category for understanding man's finitude. I would go so far as to say that it underlies all the other ways in which we spell out the difference between God's infinity and man's finitude. For our purpose here the crucial point is that the onward march of time brings man closer to death. This time before death is when man is anxious that he has to die. Tillich makes a comment which reinforces Rahner's point when he says that this anxiety is as actual in Adam as it is in Christ. In other words, this is something that is ontologically true of man and

27. Ibid., 210ff.
28. Ibid., 215.

the nature of salvation is something quite separate from this character of existence. This is why, whether or not one rejects a Wittgensteinian analysis of "immortality as meaning something other than life after death," it cannot be dismissed as nonsense. If death is natural so, as we have seen, is the fear of it. To be "half in love with easeful death" is the attitude of Romanticism. Even so it should be noted that Keats was too good a philosopher to describe himself as anything more than *half* in love and the young apothecary, knowing his medical condition as he did and remembering his brother George's death, could be forgiven for desiring an *easeful* death. The man who does not fear death is either pretending or not thinking, or is devoid of imagination. In his excellent little book *Dogmatics in Outline*,[29] Barth has a telling passage where he says that the man who does not recoil at the thought of the open grave can have very little joy in life. It is to the man who is frightened by the prospect of death and fearful of approaching it that, says Barth, the meaning of resurrection is clear. That is why the story of Jesus approaching his death given in the New Testament is not one of the simple confidence displayed by Socrates in Plato's account of the martyrdom. By contrast with Socrates Jesus agonizes in sheer terror and courageously submits.

One important feature of man's temporality is that it includes death. Contrary to Wittgenstein's claim, death *is* an event in life. This is indeed a paradox so that what Wittgenstein says is in one sense not only true but self-evidently true. Death is not lived through as an event of today that I will remember tomorrow. Death is the unique event that ends our state of pilgrimage. In a great deal of literature there is a tendency to speak of that event as a consummation; but it is only in somewhat mathematical sense that death is a consummation. It brings man's life of pilgrimage to an end in the way in which infinity brings to an end any mathematical progression. There is a finality about it that makes a man's life, whatever it may be, unalterable. Hence the old saying, "Call no man happy until he is dead." The basic decisions of a man's life here reach an end: they are made quite final. Apart from this issue of the finality of this event in life's series of events time has another significance; for death makes a man's life obviously historical and unrepeatable. Tennyson's words express the point perfectly—"the sound of a voice that is still." Do I then deny that there is in death a consummation of decision? On the contrary, I do not think that the character of death as dying is the totality of decision. I

29. Barth, *Dogmatics in Outline*, 153.

know that there are many moments of dying that come unexpected and even unknown. "He died in his sleep—how nice for him," we say; or time and again the doctor will comfort the bereaved by saying "He did not suffer anything. He did not know." For myself—pain and suffering apart—it is better to know than not to know. It is better to know because thus I decide my life finally. This is surely one of the significant features of the Passion narrative, especially in that great classical drama, the Fourth Gospel. In the Garden Jesus makes his submission—"Not my will but thine. For this I came into the world." So then we have the glorious conclusion of the story—"It is finished. Into thy hands . . ." This is the totality of the decision—no longer a decision about this or that or in favor of this rather than that but a decision about life and the world. In passing I would stress that we can speak thus only because we do not regard death as the wages of sin. One implication of this totality of death is that we do not soften the notion of death by making it refer only to a body that is separate from the *real* person, the soul. Death is a cessation of life and that is why the Christian hope uses the language of totality as it speaks of the resurrection of the body.

For Christian theology it is of paramount importance that Christ died our death. What concerns me now is not the atonement and justification he thus achieved but simply his death. His death was not merely like ours in its external aspects; his death is the very same death as ours. So the Bible and the creeds, in confessing his death, are not concerned to recite a historical fact, the datable event of the crucifixion under Pontius Pilate. As the creed goes on to say that he descended into hell so in the New Testament already there had been an anxiety to say that. Nor was that some anxiety about the pre-Christian era as is suggested by the "Enoch" reading of the verse in 1 Peter as if this were Dante's *Paradiso*. It is quite simply that after the crucifixion he was a corpse and the two days in the tomb are days when he was not part of the spatio-temporal world. His descent into hell is an essential moment of death and it establishes the substantial identity of Christ's death with our own. If the deed of his death is important so too is the fact of the resurrection. The inter-relation of the two is precisely the point that both Tillich and Bultmann in differ-ent ways grasp. For Bultmann, who would make it a myth, the resurrec-tion is—it is true—not a problem any more than it is for those who would regard it as "the best attested fact in history." Both these options seem to me to diminish the paradoxicality of the claim; for, even if we have the eye-witness accounts referred to by Paul, we do not have the peculiar event of which he speaks. As the resurrection of Christ this was no mere event; and as the resurrection of Christ it, even as an event, is one that is both in time and beyond time. The resurrection belongs as much to eternity as it does to time, "Christ dieth no more" and death has no more dominion over him. He lives; and the point of that claim is that this life is absolute and unconfined. So the Christian proclamation about death—as about everything else—is a claim about *Christ*. His self-oblation in death is the context of all our lives including our death. His death is thus our hope.

Clearly the funeral is an expression of this hope that is implied by this theology of death. The hope—we say sometimes—is of an after-life or of immortality: but here especially it is important to understand the nature of religious language. Talking about the "other side" of death as immortality is to use model language, taking as our model the mortality we know and saying "Not that but its opposite." This is the obvious and indeed the *only* kind of meaning we can give to the notion of immortality. It is impossible here to discuss the notion of the soul, but I would insist that thinking about the soul has been generated by the notion of immortality, which is then cashed out by talk about the soul. The tendency to think of the soul as some shadowy substance that is a counterpart to the body has come under very proper philosophical attack. It is a metaphysical pestilence that can generate all kinds of nonsense when people are "comforted" by being told that the spirits or souls of the departed indulge in all kinds of extraordinary activity. I would insist too that not all kinds of talk of the soul are nonsense. As Wittgenstein says, the best portrait of the soul is the body. That is precisely why the orthodox doctrine of life after death in Christianity is resurrection of the body.

Ours is indeed a time to which the Christian notion or understanding of bereavement is a gospel. Nearly a century ago Durkheim wrote about mourning as an essential social process; but only two years later Freud defined it as something essentially private. By the second half of the twentieth century the common view was that sensible, rational men and women could keep their mourning under control (and indeed that typical phraseology indicated that it was not seemly social behavior) without any need for public expression. The remarkable outburst of public sympathy and mourning after the death of Princess Diana was an extraordinary event, much of it being indeed extravagant and possibly superficial grief; but it highlighted a new readiness to *show* grief.[30] Long ago in the seventeenth century Robert Burton's *The Anatomy of Melancholy* spoke of sorrow as a cause of melancholy, giving examples of *extravagant* grief to be found in ancient texts ranging from Plutarch to the Psalms. This suggests an important distinction between melancholic mourning and grief, one made to good effect by John Ramaziani in *Poetry of Mourning*,[31] his point being that much poetry is melancholic, psychologically speaking, in that the impulse is not to achieve but to resist consolation. This is where I again find Keats so instructive. His "Ode on Melancholy" exemplifies what E. Bishop called "the art of losing," offering us as it does the bleak truth that love and loss must always coexist. The "Ode on Melancholy" takes up a theme that had been much in Keats' mind ever since his "Grecian Urn"—that art can give consolation in the face of suffering. As Andrew Motion says, "the 'Grecian Urn' is less concerned to justify or condemn an escapist aesthetic than to demonstrate the power of the imagination in general and of the negative capability in particular."[32] That balance he had struck in the "Grecian Urn" is recreated in "Ode on Melancholy." Motion says:

> This figure of Melancholy . . . is welcome yet dreadful, pleasure-giving yet embodying the same cautionary truth that Keats had previously offered at the end of the "Grecian Urn" and the "Nightingale" . . . the simultaneous apprehension of pleasure and pain that Keats had long since regarded as his ideal. But Melancholy['s] . . . consolations only exist within the confines of art.[33]

The concreteness that Keats sought is precisely the nature of the Christian hope. This concreteness of Christian hope is the mark of a Christian bereavement. There is so much more to it than the comforting thought—"They've gone to a better place." Such thoughts do not impinge on the awful sense of loss, let alone the guilt that is so often identified as the peculiar feature of bereavement. It is very easy to fall into the double trap that follows the secular attitude to death as something to be dismissed. We shuffle off death by an efficient funeral and ironically we

---

30. On bereavement see Parkes, *Bereavement: Stories of Grief in Adult Life*, and his seminal work, *Love and Loss: The Roots of Grief and its Complications*.

31. Ramaziani, *Poetry of Mourning*.

32. Motion, *Keats*, 391.

33. Ibid., 402.

adopt the fashion of calling a funeral a thanksgiving service. So we pretend that death does not really happen by pretending that the deceased is still there. But death *does* happen and bereavement is a pain that is *mine*. This is the corollary of Sartre's view that death is the triumph of the person's point of view. But as death does happen so shall the dead live in Christ. My painful bereavement is the solitude that not even hope can remove; but I can hope and that hope is for the fulfilment of which Christ's resurrection is the promise.

Appendix to Chapter 5

At the end of the lecture there was a question period during which several very interesting areas were explored. Unfortunately no record of them was made and I must depend on my memory in giving this account of the most interesting discussion. A measure of its high level of interest is that I am able to recall the vigorous exchange very clearly.

The session opened with a fundamental query about the evaluation of death given in the lecture. To the questioner it seemed that I had mistakenly presented death as an evil and had not appreciated the way in which it represented the essential balance of the universe and the great wisdom of Providence. A comparison was made between the finite length of human life and the welcome obsolescence of machines; for, it was suggested, if cars were not obsolescent and of a limited life-span then our roads would be full of cars making movement impossible. This line of argument not only has a certain quality of obvious sense but in its way could be seen as another way of emphasizing the meaningfulness of death. Yet to my mind it is only meaningfulness and good sense that we recognize in the abstract. There is very little meaning for *me* in the assertion "your disappearance and non-existence are very useful in that room is made for someone else." It is doubtless true but it is not the kind of statement that will generally seem to me relevant—I am not talking about extreme cases such as Captain Oates. Indeed, the mention of such cases of heroic self-sacrifice makes clear that this is the kind of acknowledgement that I am not likely to adopt as a general rule. True then though it is that the economy of the universe demands that life gives way to death so that new life emerges it is still true that death is perceived by us as an evil. Even if we come to accept the necessity we should still speak of it as an evil—because it is a threat and an absolute threat to my being. As I said, it is the impossibility of conceiving my own non-being that makes death so strange and terrible. Secondly, I feel that what makes death an evil is the contradiction it involves. My non-being brings to an end all that I was and ever hoped to be or could be. Once again I am reminded of Keats' graphic description of ambition unfulfilled and this finds an instant echo in the way we speak of him cut off in his prime. Had he not died he would have been the second Shakespeare of English literature. We think of Bonhoeffer and the great unfinished work on *Ethics* smuggled out of prison before he was murdered by his Nazi jailers and we will say "What great theology this would have been." Bring it nearer home and we remember the young medical student killed in the Lockerbie air disaster. Our reaction is the same—"How much she could have achieved in Medicine," we will say of something that never will be. Nor is the contradiction merely that between promise and the frustration of fulfillment. There is a contradiction of what we see as the fundamental reasonableness of life and we speak of them as a waste or a shame, something incomprehensible. It is very easy here to fall into one of two very different errors—to sentimentalize the tragedy or, on the other hand, treat it in an abstractly intellectual fashion. What we can neither sentimentalize nor reduce to abstraction is the moral life and it is clear to all of us that our moral advance, such as it is, will be cut short by death. Reference was made in the lecture to the way in which the philosopher Kant plumbed the depths of the human conscience and spoke so tellingly of faith in those terms. The contrast between what I am and what I ought to be, the gap in between whatever I can muster of goodness and the perfection of moral life commanded, was so clear to Kant that he based his argument of immortality on that premises. None of us can afford to say that we do not need tomorrow in order to try and achieve the virtue we have so far failed to achieve. It is crucial that we appreciate what we are saying here; for I am not in any way making claims about the importance or significance of an individual life but pointing to the sovereignty of good in any life. So—to return to the point—if it is indeed sovereign and is in fact achievable then what prevents its achievement must be evil.

The second question raised the problem of the relevance of near-death experiences to our understanding of the meaning of death. Did they not seem the very kind of evidence we needed if we wanted either a definition of death or even only a better understanding of what it would be? More attractive still seemed the possibility of gleaning from these sources information not only about death itself but also about our passage through it to what lies beyond. While confessing my very limited knowledge of what is now a very extensive and popularly acclaimed body of evidence I answered this question by urging caution. What strikes me about this kind of evidence is its essential dubiety as being by its very nature private experience. We are utterly dependent on the narrator of this private experience in exactly the same way as we are for knowing what people dream. As in the case of dreams, where the relation of the physical and the psychological is so mysterious and yet so intrinsic that we are prone to say such things as "I always dream after cheese," so here it is difficult to say just what the evidence signifies. In any case the analogy with dreams shows how this kind of experience cannot function as evidence; for, as the philosopher Hobbes said, "If a man says to me that God spoke to him in a dream I will say that he dreamt that God spoke to him." Moreover, the whole point of many of these stories was in fact that they expressed the narrator's faith. It was not the experience that generated that faith but the lively faith in "the hand outstretched caressingly," as Francis Thompson said, which made the experience what it is.

The third question was another direct engagement with one of the lecture's themes, asking how sudden death would be an expression of freedom. This does seem so direct and devastating a challenge to the way I described death that one might be tempted to retreat and say that death is not always this final act of freedom. It is obvious that death can come not only unexpectedly but instantly and possibly without our being aware of it. If it seems difficult to speak of an act of freedom in regard to something instantaneous it is surely impossible to regard an unconscious action as an expression of freedom. Was I then exaggerating or being over-romantic in what I said about death? I do not think so and the force of the criticism lies in the simplistic view of human freedom. When I spoke of death as the final act of freedom I was not saying that the end of my life is this event of my final act of freedom as if there were something beyond my dying. Nor was I saying that it is never the case that death is something that happens to me rather than something I do. There are indeed two issues here rather than one. First, it is important to understand that when I say of my action that it is something I choose to do I am not thereby indicating another event besides the event in question. The other point is that talk about freedom is talk about my responsibility and what I am emphasizing by saying that death is the final act of freedom is that I am responsible for my progress up to that point. If we think of the way that St. John makes Jesus talk of his death it shows the two points very well. "I am laying it down of my own free will," he says of his sacrificial death. Just as that laying it down is his free choice so too that is the responsibility he has exercised and still does at the point of his death. As the last definable point in which I can be spoken of in this way death then signifies the summation of those possibilities. "He never knew who he was," says Biff of his dead father in *Death of a Salesman*—precisely because in that life and at that death such a decisively free action had been possible. The puzzle of the question is precisely the mystery of a free act that, as I said, is not something that can be reported in the newspapers.

A particularly difficult question was raised concerning freedom from an entirely different angle—the problem of suicide, several aspects of which were raised in a striking way. Is not suicide the most dramatic example of death as a free act? And in the burial of a suicide what freedom does the pastor have other than the acknowledgement of that act of freedom? While it would have been impossible to deal with all the relevant issues it seemed to me that this thorny problem should be firmly grasped and that there were three important parts to any proper answer. In the first place, there is the general issue of freedom in a world created by an omnipotent, loving God; for suicide can never be anything but tragedy. The most chilling lines in *Hedda Gabler* are her question about the suicide—"Did he do it beautifully?" Anyone who has known a case of suicide in the story of a friend or relative knows the extreme burden of sorrow, a sorrow in particular about one's own failure to have done something to relieve this tragedy. That raises in a most poignant way the traditional problem of evil—how God's almighty love can compass this. Answering that question is clearly impossible in a small space even if it is possible to answer it at all. Yet in one rather brutal sense the assertion of the fundamental worth and importance of human freedom is the end of the matter. We cannot have a world in which man has the divine quality of freedom without there being the possibility of rejecting the very gift of life itself. This is but one feature of Milton's picture of Lucifer's fall and yet perhaps it is even more awe-ful than the terrible and defiant pride we associate with "Better to reign in Hell . . ." Freedom carries with it the possibility of subverting life itself. Secondly, it is worth recalling the traditional view of suicide as a grave if not the gravest sin—a sin against God as Creator and Redeemer, a rejection of His love and a denial of His sovereignty, and an offence against one's own person as made in the image of God, which renders impossible any act of repentance. Therefore, ecclesiastical law refused to allow Christian burial to any suicide. It is perhaps an indication of a greater charity that there has been little discussion of the issue in the last thirty years. Our concern at the moment, however, is with the nature of the act itself and it is in that context that I find this view very revealing. It seems to me that what earns the special degree of opprobrium from traditional moralists is the nature of this act as *more than* killing. It is because I kill *myself* not because I contravene the Sixth Commandment that this is deemed so grievous a sin. Interestingly enough it was precisely this self-reference of the volition that made it for Sartre something inconceivable. As I said, it is seen as an offence against God the Creator: its specially offensive quality as such is that it is a negation of that very act of God in creating. This is why I thought that Milton's phrase "Better to reign in Hell . . ." had a special mysterious force; for here what is going on is not a case of settling for the second-best as when we shall content ourselves with good late-bottled instead of vintage port or a lithograph instead of a Kyffin Williams oil painting. This is a matter of conceiving negativity and destruction as if it were of equal value with the positive and the created. If, as Wittgenstein said, in death my world ceases then indeed suicide is the attempt to do the very opposite of what God does as Creator—and this is not only to set myself up as equal to Him but it is also very obviously rejecting what He values and what He is. Glanville Williams notes the relevance of the paradox that "if one person can lawfully commit suicide why should it be an offence for another to help him?" and the suggestion is that "we still think suicide immoral."[34] The third point relates to the pastoral situation envisaged. Here, I think, the issue is a simple demand for compassion; and this works in two ways. First, I have no right to sit in judgement on a fellow human being because in everything it is true that but for the grace of God I would fall again and again with the self-same sin repeated a hundredfold. I have not the right because I cannot tell the exact circumstances and so any strictly just evaluation is impossible. Secondly, in so far as this has happened to a fellow human being it has happened to me, as John Donne's famous words make so clear. It will indeed be true that my friend is beyond my service and it may even be the case that his family is also; but his memory is still something that calls for my compassion.

The very last question was rather a difficult one because it concerned issues of Scripture and doctrine raised with regard to what had been said about the language of death. Why, it was asked, did I say that one could

---

34. Glanville Williams, *Textbook on Criminal Law*, 531.

not say "I have died," that this expression was linguistically impossible when this is exactly the kind of thing that the book of Revelation puts in the mouth of Christ? Once again any full treatment would be long and complicated—not least because one would have to begin with the critical questions about the text. Perhaps the most relevant point in that context is that this is visionary literature so that there would be an analogy in my dreaming about my own funeral and so witnessing it. Even, however, if we take the words at their face value I do not think this makes me change what I said. True though it is that we can speak of Christ's resurrection as the first fruits of them that sleep that basis of our most certain hope is a *unique* event. In saying this I am not indulging in any outmoded Christology from above, talking as if Christ were some Greek god masquerading as a human being. The point is that any Christology, including one that starts with the hard fact of the history of Jesus of Nazareth, must speak of the glorification of him who died. The essential mystery of the Christian faith is that it proclaims the efficacy of the salvation wrought by Christ's death and resurrection with reference to what is for us seen as nothing other than an end.

Chapter 6

Responsibility as an Inclusive Concept

The various political problems or scandals that have made front page news in national and even international newspapers of late have all been concerned with identifying responsibility for actions. While politicians have exercised their casuistical skills in scoring points or claiming the high moral ground the natural platform for the latter has usually been assumed to be the Christian church. However, the ascription of responsibility is neither the sole possession nor indeed the distinctive activity of Christians. It would seem to be indisputable that moral judgment of any kind presupposes and employs the notion of responsibility. Thus, commenting on the Shakespearean contempt for nature, Gadamer remarks that for Shakespeare the human conscience makes man responsible for his actions. If we turn back to St. Thomas Aquinas it is instructive that in the first article of the moral part of *Summa Theologiae*[1] Thomas says that moral acts and human acts are the same, having said previously that "only those acts which proceed from deliberate will are properly called human actions."[2] That is to say, if we describe an act as a human act then we can hold the agent responsible for it. Thus, though the conception of morality as obedience to divine will, which had predominated before the seventeenth century, gave way in this and the succeeding centuries to a different understanding of morality as self-governance, throughout this history of the varying understanding of morality responsibility is a constant among the variables. It could be argued that even in the medieval discussion of the issues of soteriology responsibility had been taken to be a necessary element of moral thinking. An even better example than

1. Aquinas, *Summa Theologiae*, 1a 11ae q.1.a.3.
2. Ibid., a.1.

the framework of St. Anselm's view of atonement in *Cur Deus Homo* is afforded by his *De Casu Diaboli* when he asks whether God could escape responsibility for the Devil's sin. If the Devil had known that obedience was the greatest good he would not have fallen. That ignorance could not have been the Devil's choice and so God could be said to be responsible for the fall. That Anselm does not accept that conclusion is irrelevant, the point being that for Anselm responsibility is a key issue with regard to moral action, even God's.[3] What I shall try to do in this chapter is to consider how a sociological understanding of responsibility relates to the moral concept and whether we can speak of the notion in theological ethics "including" the sociological. Thus, the argument of William Schweiker's *Responsibility and Christian Ethics* is that "theological ethics must be understood in terms of an integrated theory," a theory of responsibility which is grounded in an analysis of human life and relations and sees the source of responsibility in God. His conclusion is that the Christian faith claims that the basic moral experience that it is good to exist "is a testimony to the fact that we live, move, and have our being in God."[4]

Let us begin with the trivial observation that the subject matter of theology seems to have something in common with that of sociology in that both inquire into the forms that shape and sustain communal life and both inquire systematically into the nature and fulfilment of such life. It could also be said that, without the correction of empirical investigation, theological ethics falls into a formalism that is justly condemned as being so heavenly that it has no earthly use. Yet it is also true that the theologian who looks at the social sciences will be inclined to feel that social science dissipates its energies all too easily in sheer empiricism, missing what are to him the real questions that a study such as this ought to raise—questions about man's achievements and his destiny. Furthermore, the two disciplines take radically different perspectives on man and the pattern of his life. Although both are concerned with man, theological ethics investigates those patterns that guide man's actions in a non-empirical way and towards non-empirical goals whereas the social sciences inquire into those patters or structures that can be isolated as causes or causal factors in the development of which we speak. Clearly, if these are said to be the only real structures the theologian and the social scientist part

3. See Anselm, *Anselm of Canterbury*, vol. 2, 139ff.
4. Schweiker, *Responsibility and Christian Ethics*, 227.

company at once. The problem can be formulated in a more specific way if we concentrate on the divergence of opinion about man. What the theologian contends is that in giving an account of man's behavior and decisions in terms of the pressures that are inherent in the particular structures of society to which the sociologist has related these events the sociologist has denied to man any responsibility for affecting change. I turn then to this concept of responsibility.

The concept of responsibility is not unique to either ethics or theology: that, in a sense, is what constitutes our problem. If not actually borrowed from the sphere of law the notion of responsibility is a fundamentally legal notion and it might even be said that, as used in ethics, it is a metaphor: which is why the relation with the fundamentally metaphorical thought-world of theology is so interesting. "Responsible" means—as its etymology suggests—"answerable." Every citizen is legally responsible, answerable to the nation's law and answerable for this or that. He is answerable to an authority that can compel him to do his duty, to respect his neighbor's rights, or else to pay the penalty prescribed by law. Someone is responsible *for* Y when Y is a factor in a duty or the duty itself or the action that is the default in respect of a duty. Tesco food stores are responsible for the Pork Pies they make, for seeing that they are edible and comply with the Public Health requirements when they are sold and again for the whole condition of the sale of the pie to me. Thus they are responsible for my being sold a Melton Mowbray pie when it was not in fact made in Melton Mowbray, Leicestershire. So responsibility in the legal sense then need not be a responsibility for some particular thing; but in all cases it means that either I did X or that someone else who was my agent did X and that doing X infringes somebody's right. So far it is a clear matter of what is involved in the law of the land. However, a person may be said to be morally responsible though he or she has in no way fallen foul of the law. Consider the case of the missing son who returns in James Hilton's *Random Harvest*. The father dies without including him in the will because he was unaware that his son was in fact alive. Despite the fact that there is no provision for him in the will the missing son, argues the family lawyer, is entitled to his proper share of the family fortune. The strict application of the law does not require this; but, despite themselves, the family members are persuaded that they are *morally* responsible to do this. This is a very clear illustration of the way in which we make a distinction between moral and legal responsibility, seeing the former as more extensive than the latter.

The preceding argument is very interesting when we ask what it is for the notion of responsibility to be said to be inapplicable or for the ascription of responsibility to be false. Aristotle sees the ascription of responsibility for an action to be liable to defeat in two ways. Someone cannot be said to be responsible for X if X was done by compulsion or it was done through ignorance. With regard to the latter he says that only when the agent can show that he was ignorant of the conditions or circumstances that affect the morality of the action is responsibility defeated.[5] The notion of defeat is used rather differently by H. L. A. Hart,[6] who takes the term from the law of property and extends its meaning. In the law of property, he says, it is used to refer to an estate or legal interest in land "which is subject to termination or 'defeat' in a number of different contingencies but remains intact if no such contingencies mature."[7] He extends the meaning to cover all legal claims that are regarded as provisionally established at a certain stage of the litigation process but still vulnerable to defeat, annulment, or revocation at some later stage of the proceedings. Defeasibility in this sense then would seem to be what we would regard as the inherent nature of a *prima facie* case. That said, it is worth pointing out that in order to establish a *prima facie* case proof must be established by the plaintiff. In other words, there is an important difference between this notion of *prima facie* and the way in which W. D. Ross spoke of *prima facie* duty and what we might then speak of as a *prima facie* responsibility. Here the context is the adversarial system of litigation with its complex of rules. The sufficiency of legal claims and the nature of evidence are necessary *defined* features of a *prima facie* case being established. That there are some very revealing analogies between this and the ascription of moral responsibility does not abrogate the important difference. If, for instance, we consider the dominical injunction that we should not judge lest we be judged then the implication would be that the process of judgment cannot begin. However, the injunction clearly presupposed the fact of a judgment, the relevance of which is what should govern any judgment that I make. Failure to make clear a distinction between legal and moral responsibility has been one of the main sources of confusion about the notion of freedom. It is clear that in some sense or other responsibility presupposes

5. See Lucas, *Responsibility*, 275.

6. Hart, "The Ascription of Responsibility and Right."

7. Ibid., 175.

freedom—hence Kant's dictum "I ought, therefore I can." Here, of course, it is important to be aware of the width of meaning "responsibility" has because responsibility for some faults is obviously defeasible. It is surely a fault in a tyre that it has no tread and similarly a moldy pie is a faulty pie. When we attribute such defects to tyres or pies we leave no room for the reply that the tyre has travelled 50,000 miles or that the pie was kept in inadequate refrigeration. Similarly faulty appearance and faulty intelligence are equally clear examples of non-defeasible faults. And though a faulty character is a more difficult problem yet tactlessness and lack of humor are things that can be forgiven, regretted, or even deplored *but* not denied. What is clear is that defeasibility is problematic only when we are considering what St. Thomas Aquinas talked of as specifically *human acts*.

It is interesting that when we judge acts we do regard some character faults as clearly defeasible. There are surely cases where the imputation of wickedness can be defeated utterly. We might say that what seemed to be pure wickedness was in fact a result of a neurotic compulsion. The father who tries to kill his children and himself is said to be not responsible for his action and in need of psychiatric care rather than prosecution for murder. A less difficult example is the charge of cruelty being defeated by the evidence of mistaken beliefs so that we use the rather odd expression that it was a case of "unknowing cruelty." What is true of character is true also of action. "He broke the window" seems non-defeasible whereas "he broke faith with his friend" seems defeasible. If what he did was done by mistake or accident it cannot properly be called "breaking faith." What, then, is the basis of the distinction between defeasible and non-defeasible ascriptions of responsibility for faulty performance? The broken window is a simple fact and if that results from an equally simple action on the part of the agent then it is non-defeasible. If, however, the person who broke the window had been pushed or had fallen in an epileptic fit then this is defeasible. Doing the right thing may be a simple fact; but whether it is done for the wrong reason raises the question of responsibility. Both defeasible and non-defeasible ascriptions of responsibility *express* blame but the defeasible ascription raises the doubt whether there is revealed some volition that is in some sense extraneous to the mere faultiness of the action. What was said earlier about moral and legal responsibility will suggest that although it would not be true to say that all the verbs in defeasible ascriptions always express moral condemnation, they do express value-judgments, and these, as Hare pointed out, entail imperatives.[8]

I am morally responsible for the choices I make at particular times in specific situations when these choices are not themselves determined by environment or anything else. I am morally responsible only when I am absolutely free in the sense that though everything else remained the same my action could have been different. It does not in the least follow that I am morally responsible for doing something which is an impossibility. What is implied is that there can be no purely general description of the circumstances in which moral responsibility is ascribed in that they will vary with the individual concerned. There are, for example, many things that I am not tempted to do—something for which one is grateful. I am not tempted to forge cheques, to defraud, to be cruel to animals, to deprive men of their means of livelihood, *but* I am tempted in other ways. C. P. Snow's *The Masters* is an excellent study of the kinds of temptation that a man in the scholar's ivory tower faces. What is perhaps the most important point here is that we read Snow's story as a tale about human choices and human characters so that our final evaluation of the action is in that sense a moral rather than a sociological judgment. I can take no credit from not succumbing to those temptations that do not attract me; but I can take moral credit for resisting those temptations that I really face. Without entering into any exegesis of "Lead us not into temptation" we can say that there is no fault in being exposed to temptation, as is very clear from the whole discussion of Christ's sinlessness. What matters morally is how I behave when I have to fulfill duties too great for my character. The old Welsh song (*Plas Gogerddan*) describes a youth fleeing from the battlefield and being urged by his mother to return and fight alongside his father with the words "I'd rather see you dead than see you live as a coward." Moral worth, then, is measured by the effort we make, or fail to make, to resist temptation, particularly when the temptation challenges our weakness of character or what Aristotle calls *akrasia*, weakness of will.[9] This is why we describe moral responsibility as par excellence a defeasible ascription. This too is why religious views of responsibility stress not only the responsibility of the individual but the difficulty if not impossibility of properly judging anyone else. Only God and the individual himself know fully—and, like Augustine, the

8. Hare, *Language of Morals*, 167ff.

9. Aristotle, *Nichomachean Ethics* VII, 1ff.

individual agent might confess that he or she does not fully know—how a man acquits himself in any situation. I would not say that this is what the dominical injunction "Judge not" (Matt 7:1) *means* but this is certainly part of it.

Furthermore, the impossibility of judging implies that there is a sense in which moral responsibility is enlarged or heightened in the context of religion. The concept of responsibility is obviously stretched in such sayings as "When ye shall have done all those things which are commanded you, say 'We are unprofitable servants'" (Luke 17:10). The remainder of the verse only heightens the paradox. If the fulfilment of duty leaves a responsibility for something else we cannot be using the terms in their normal moral sense. Yet, the religious consciousness recognizes that there is a sense: as Kierkegaard says, there is edification in the thought that as against God we are *always* in the wrong.[10] Though it is not immediately relevant it is interesting to note that Kierkegaard dealt with this theme three times. The first time is in the book *Repetition* where Job asserts his righteousness before God but finally has to recognize his unrighteousness. The second time is in the last portion of *Either-Or*, "Ultimatum," with the discourse "The Edification in the thought that in relation to God we are always in the wrong," man's unrighteousness is even more strongly emphasized. The same theme occurs again in the third part of *Upbuilding Discourses*, but from a higher point of view. Here there is no more talk of wrong, only of guilt, in relation to God. The meaningfulness of this paradox is strongly argued by Levinas when he talks of the infinity of ethics and says "At no time can one say: I have done all my duty."[11] To return to Kierkegaard, it was with these thoughts that he consoled himself when in his anguish he was at the point of revolting against God. Not to recognize that in our relation to God we are always unrighteous is, he thought, the same as trying to abolish God. If a theological objection is made to the effect that Kierkegaard thus neglects grace this is to misunderstand his emphasis. As he says in his *Journal*, "I will present the Christian demand—discipleship—in all its infiniteness in order to thrust the individual in the direction of grace."[12] Elsewhere in his *Journal*, toward the end of his life, he wrote, "And what is the sum total of what I

---

10. Kierkegaard, *Either-Or* 2, 335–54.
11. E Levinas, *Ethics and Infinity*, 105
12. Kierkegaard, *Papirer*, X5 A 88.

have done? Quite simply, I have injected just a little bit of *honesty*."[13] Presenting Christianity honestly was to describe the frightening character of its *infinite* demand. Kierkegaard thus clearly shows how the religious concept of responsibility involves our seeing it in the context of a higher ethic in the sense that however rigorous the secular ethic is responsibility here gains greater force—seen as something absolute because of its infinite context.

This suggestion of a higher ethic reminds one that there is what C. A. Mace called a "network of interlacing hierarchies" within which each one of us has his distinctive position. In his article "Hierarchical Organization" he writes:

> It is doubtful whether at any point in man's development or history, the individual can properly be described as a member of an undifferentiated herd, but the further he departs from this and the more he come to occupy a position in the network of interlacing hierarchies the less adequate merely general psychological principles become for the interpretation of his behaviour and his inner mental life. At the levels with which the sociologist is in the main concerned with him, all his reactions are the expression of the attitudes and ties which his position entails. The "struggle for existence" has become "the pursuit of a career"—a more or less regularized progression through hierarchical ranks, the successive steps of which are conditioned by seniority, experience and the satisfaction of semi-automatic tests. Pugnacity has become litigation or the operation of "machinery of conciliation." The instinct to escape is no longer invoked by the perils of the jungle, but by the threatened loss of status. The basic social processes of suggestion, sympathy . . . now descend downwards and outwards, through defined hierarchical channels.[14]

Here Mace is emphasizing the importance of contextual setting just as much as the moralist does; but the context for him is society. Does this mean that when we look for the context for our judgments about human behavior the social context affords all the hierarchy of which we have spoken so far? What Peter Winch says about the personal participation involved in social behavior is very instructive: it is participation of a distinctive kind. "Voting," for instance, is not merely a matter of marking bits of paper and putting them into boxes as part of an exercise to keep

---

13. Kierkegaard, *Papirer*, XI 1 A 474.
14. Mace, "Hierarchical Organization," 391–92.

psychologists in a job. When N "votes" his "act must be a participation in the political life of the country, which presupposes that he must be aware of the symbolic relation between what he is doing now and the government which comes to power after the election."[15]

Winch makes another very significant point when he says that certain sociologists fail to realize that the kind of "law" that the sociologist may formulate to account for the behavior of human beings is logically different from a "law" in natural science. The same sort of point can be made about the predilection of some sociologists for what is called "single-factor" or "key-cause" theories. Causal ascriptions show the same kind of vulnerability as the defeasibility of legal claims and accusations. When a humanly interesting event occurs it is always possible to mention dozens of factors that have made important causal contributions to its occurrence. There is something very arbitrary about the assertion that one of these is *the* cause of any situation or event. There has been and there will continue to be much discussion about Tony Blair's decision to support the invasion of Iraq. Despite the ready accusation of a messianic complex made by more than one critic, judicious biographers have seen Blair's publicly acknowledged Christian faith as constituting more of a paradox than an explanation. In general, causal ascriptions commit the error not of misdescribing a situation but of representing the less important as the more important. Winch refers to Popper who, he says, "explicitly compares" what he does for the social sciences "to the construction of theoretical models in the natural sciences."[16] Popper says in his *Poverty of Historicism*:

> The use of models explains and at the same time destroys the claims of methodological essentialism; . . . it explains them, for the model is of an abstract or theoretical character, and we are liable to believe that we see it . . . as a kind of observable ghost or essence and it destroys them because our task is to analyse our sociological models carefully . . . in *terms of individuals*.[17]

With this kind of scepticism Winch would have agreed; but he thought that Popper's characterization of social institutions as explanatory models introduced by the social scientist for his own purposes is grievously wrong. However, Winch's point is that Popper allows for no

15. Winch, *The Idea of a Social Science*, 51.
16. Ibid.
17. Popper, *Poverty of Historicism*, sec. 29.

genuine social community, no genuine social relations, no distinctive social interaction between men. What he would argue is that Popper's models have done scant justice to the distinctively social character of what social studies study. This means that giving a sociological account requires the use of a variety of possible models.

It might be thought that we are moving too easily to some kind of accommodation. It could be argued that however much sociology is developed as a distinctively human study that there will always remain a tension between it and theology. Sociology, according to Karl Mannheim, is a secularized, perhaps the most secularized approach to the problem of human life. Yet one lesson that we could be said to have learned in the twentieth century is that there can be no simple contrast between secular and religious life. Just as one of the most important achievements of Winch's book was that it reminded us that intellectual ideas and outlook are necessary parts of a sociological phenomenon so Tillich emphasized in the third volume of his *Systematic Theology* that the church is a sociologically determined group. The importance of Winch's argument is that *as sociology* an account of religious behavior must do justice to the religious character of what we study. "A monk," he says, "has certain characteristic social relations with his fellow monks and with people outside the monastery; but it would be impossible to give more than a superficial account of those relations without taking into account the religious ideas around which the monk's life revolves."[18]

One problem that remains is that of the agent described as mentally ill. If we regard responsibility as the correlative of motive can we say that, for example, the kleptomaniac is responsible for his actions? The point is that if we were applying a scientific model of impulse and resistance it would be very difficult to distinguish between this case and some quite blameless case of the pursuit of some particular goal of gratification. Yet it is clear that we should not be as ready to *blame* the kleptomaniac as we would be to blame the common thief; and the kinds of sophisticated thefts that have made headline news regarding pension frauds and other financial scandals will readily evoke moral condemnation and the people concerned are said to be responsible, something we have hesitated to say in the case of the kleptomaniac. What is nevertheless important to make clear is that the greater clemency shown does not entirely remove the propriety of ascribing responsibility. The general rule that the criminal

18. Ibid., 23.

is a morally culpable person is not in any way weakened by the fact that when we apportion blame we do take into account the forces of circumstance that are against the agent. This includes what was said earlier about weakness of will. A common plea that the counsellor or confessor will hear is "With my character I could not have done otherwise." What is evident here is the need for caution in our exercise of moral condemnation. If I may apply Tillich's famous Protestant Principle in a context other than his own, what this means is that theological analyses of situations and ascriptions of responsibility cannot proceed as if they had a clear structural vision of the whole. What is interesting is that this humility is corroborated by sociological inquiries into the changing character of the whole. Even so, it cannot be too strongly emphasized that on sociology too there is enjoined a similar humility. We have seen that a religious conception of responsibility involves not only those models whereby we describe empirical situations but also those models that enable us to discern the mystery of the whole, the mystery of our ignorance of our relatedness and our betrayal of love. I have also argued that though the sociologist might imagine that his task is relatively straightforward it too involves a variety of models and in that sense is no less complicated. For the Christian the world is God's creation, and this faith has epistemological as well as cosmological significance. It has to do, that is, with what it is that one knows and how one knows it, as well as with what exists. That one's knowledge of factual reality depends on this faith is something that was very clear to Descartes as he elaborated his arguments concerning knowledge. So value and fact are reconciled in the assertion of the reality of God not simply as elements of the definition of the believer's behavior in the world. The Christian sees himself or herself as both responsible *to God* and *before God* for action, both individual and social, in God's world.

The relevance of what has just been said to the theme of our discussion is that if we argue thus then we are saying that the notion of responsibility in theological ethics does not merely transcend the sociological or even the ethical concept but it actually includes both. Such an understanding was what moved H. Richard Niebuhr to give his Robertson Lecture on "The Responsible Self," the sub-title "An Essay in Christian Moral Philosophy." We are told by his son in the Preface to the book published posthumously in 1963 that his father "had poured the largest part of his energies" into the "fundamental architectonic ideas of the discipline of systematic ethics."[19] Towards the end of the book Richard Niebuhr says:

> In practice, Christians undertaking to act in conformity with Christ find themselves doing something like what some others, conforming to other images, are doing. Identity of action there has not been; likeness, however, has often been present. . . . For the most part these affinities of the Christian ethos with other types of universal ethics have been stated in terms of idealism or of legalism.[20]

The point about images could start our discussion anew; but there is another point that we can usefully note. It is significant that the two types of similar ethics Niebuhr noted are idealism and legalism. What is characteristic of idealism is that it refuses to ground ethics in the natural while legalism will insist that ethics is characterized by the notion of obligation. It is a small step from the former to saying that ethics is grounded in the transcendent divine behind the natural. Likewise it is an equally small step from the latter position to saying that I have obligations because I have a duty to God. Niebuhr himself points to the significance of his definition of these ethics as universal when he goes on to say that:

> The ethic of Jesus Christ, as the way of life of one who responds to the action of the universal God in all actions, in whatever happens, is an ethic of universal responsibility and not wholly alien to all those styles of life that men have developed when they have lifted up their eyes beyond the particularities of their situation and looked for the universal good beyond all special goods, the universal law beyond all local law, the universal action beyond all particular action.[21]

It would be very easy to dismiss this as a particular rhetorical flourish were it not for the fact that the rhetoric echoes the way in which each of the concepts displays the idealization that makes it impossible to analyze them into particular natural judgments.

In conclusion I return to Kierkegaard. One of the greatest and indeed fundamental misinterpretations of his thought is the view that his idea of ethics (and of religion) is that of an essentially interior affair. A typical *Journal* entry gives the lie to this—"Christianity is nothing but

19. Richard Niebuhr, *The Responsible Self*, 1.

20. Ibid., 168.

21. Ibid., 172.

religion right in the middle of life and weekdays."[22] It is true that he is very emphatic on the internal source of the ethic of love, as when he says in *Works of Love* that it has its source deep in the heart of man. Yet he was just as clear in his condemnation of the mistaken view of his fellow-Lutherans that it was something purely hidden. This is the biting comment he offers in his *Journal*:

> With the gradual decrease of concern for being an authentic Christian and of enthusiasm through actually being that, and since on the other hand people did not wish to break completely with Christianity, hidden inwardness arose. Hidden inwardness excuses one from actual renunciation, excuses one from all the inconvenience of suffering for the cause of Christianity. This was agreed to and on this condition men continued to be Christian—it was convenient.[23]

The interest and relevance of Kierkegaard is that, while he was very much aware of the variety of motifs in Christian ethics, it was for him basically an ethic of obligation. Thus the argument of *Works of Love* is quite simply that the Christian ethic is an ethic of divine command and the command is "Thou shalt love thy neighbor," the first three parts of it taking up and stressing each element in turn. It is an ethic of command—Thou *shalt*; it is an ethic that is obviously directed towards the other—the *neighbor*; and it is a command that is addressed to each and every individual—*Thou* shalt love. Responsibility in *Works of Love* is essentially a practical matter: we are called, says Kierkegaard, to be aware of our eternal responsibility before God in a practical way. That eternal relation puts our relation to our neighbor in a new light; for we are now committed to the debt of love to other people, and that is a countless or infinite debt. To argue thus is not to make morality dependent on religion but rather to show how a hierarchical understanding of responsibility makes sense of a theological ethic, sense that does not make nonsense of secular ethics.

22. Kierkegaard, *Papirer*, X3 A 51.

23. Kierkegaard, *Journals and Papers*, vol. 2, 466–67; Kierkegaard, *Papirer* X3 A 434.

Chapter 7

Global Life and Death

So far we have looked at personal life and death. Now I want to suggest that theology's characteristic concern with the doctrines of the last things, the end of the world, puts it in a special position of relevance to an age that can conceive of an imminent end. When I was a boy it was quite usual for one to see—on a Saturday night invariably—someone walking up and down the main street of the town carrying a banner with the message "The end is nigh." For us as children this was funny; and when I was a teenager I thought it was an irrelevance or worse. Prophecies of the end struck all of us as pieces of idiosyncracy. Now, however, as we have entered a new millennium millennial doom is in the air. Global warming and nuclear proliferation—not to mention the ever volatile political situation and miseries of the Eastern Hemisphere—are issues which have impinged on everyone's experience. As I have said, we are an age that *speaks* of an *end*: even the notion of post-something is now itself passé. When I was a student one was excited by Karl Mannheim's work and came to bandy about the notion that the twentieth century was a "post-Christian era." That, as well as post-modernism, post-history, or (to borrow George Steiner's term) post-culture—we are beyond all this. The sun, we felt, was about to set on the era that is post-industrial or post-modern or whatever. The latest eschatological craze gave rise to this talk of an end. The philosopher A. C. Danto spoke of "the end of art" and a Washington journal, *National Interest*, carried as a lead article one by Francis Fukuyama entitled "The End of History?" Fukuyama's work became so popular and so much noticed (noticed perhaps more than critically understood) that predictably enough it evoked an equally provocative response by France's leading theorist of post-modernism, Jean Baudrillard, who argued in his book, *The Illusion of the End*, that the notion of the end is part of what he regarded as the phantasy of linear history. On that particular issue I do no more at the moment than refer back to what was said earlier (chapter 2): this understanding of history as indeed a function of time is one of the great contributions of Christian faith to human understanding. As some critics responded to the Fukuyama affair by talking of "endism" the truth was that we were rewriting the twentieth century, being engaged in a gigantic process of historical revisionism; and we were in a hurry to finish it before the actual end of the century, secretly hoping to be able to begin again from scratch.

It is worth staying for a moment with Fukuyama since that helps us to focus the theological problem. His interpretation of history clearly is based somewhat loosely on the views of Hegel. It is something of a cliché to say that Hegel introduced the subject of history into philosophy. What is certainly true is that in the Hegelian system everything is peculiarly historicized. As Kierkegaard saw, Hegelianism was marked by two emphases—the rationality of the real and the dialectical structure of progress. Only the rational was real and progress occurred through opposition—with the guarantee that divine Reason would realize itself through history. As I said, this is the view on which Fukuyama loosely bases his understanding of history. According to him, history is a long struggle to realize the idea of freedom, which is latent in human consciousness. In the twentieth century the forces of totalitarianism have been decisively conquered by the U.S. and its allies, which represent the final embodiment of this idea—"that is, the endpoint of mankind's ideological evolution and the universalization of Western liberal democracy. So the end of history is good news rather than bad news." Fukuyama is not too sure; for he finds an "emptiness at the core of liberalism." The society Hegel envisioned as that of the end of history was a universal state in which the arts flourish and virtue reigns. What we find, however, is a "consumerist culture" purveying pop music and trendy boutique goods all over the world. There are two points that I want to carry forward from this account of the article: (a) that our Western liberal culture is consumerist and so creates artificial demands on our world (b) that contemporary experience presses on everyone the notion of an end with all the foreboding of disaster that traditionally has been associated with the phrase "end of the world."

As the issues of ecology and its interrelation with political stability and economic industrial development came to the fore in the closing years of the twentieth century so theology became poised to recover some of its lost interests. The problem of the pollution of rivers like the Rhine, the Tyne, and the Thames and of seas like the Mediterranean, which had been described as "a sewer for centuries," the problem of acid rain and the defoliation and indeed destruction of forests, the global effects of nuclear accidents like Chernobyl—these are all well-known concerns of recent history. The debate reached a high point in 1972 with two publications. The January issue of *The Ecologist* published a *Blueprint for Survival* advocating, amongst other things, a reduction in the population of Britain from fifty-three million to thirty million so that it could live off its own agricultural resources and thereafter maintain a stable society with zero population and economic growth. The other was the Club of Rome's *The Limits to Growth* produced by D. H. Meadows and others. Using computer predictions of dynamic interactions between population, food production, pollution, the level of industrial activity, and the consumption of non-renewable natural resources it stressed the danger of growth by a constant percentage of a whole over a period of time. They give the example of lilies in a pond that double themselves daily; if they could cover the pond in thirty days on the twenty-ninth they would still only half cover it. So on this assumption the world would move quickly from a situation of abundance to one of crisis. Unless drastic changes were made, it was argued, by the year 2100 we would have the end of civilization. Further reports from the Club of Rome, such as *Mankind at the Turning Point* (1975), *Reshaping the International Order* (1977), and *Goals for Mankind* (also of 1977), have modified the analysis and predictions but have only served to heighten our awareness of "the ecological crisis." Thus it is argued that the problem is not so much growth in itself as undifferentiated growth—undifferentiated as distinct from stable, organic growth; and further it is suggested that we need to concentrate on the north-south divide. The problems of pollution and famine must, it is said, be left for future generations to solve. This hard counsel and bleak prospect were the clearest indications that we were indeed faced with an "ecological crisis."

In 1989 Margaret Thatcher shocked the United Nations with a speech that warned of a new "insidious danger," "the prospect of irretrievable damage to the atmosphere, to the ocean, to the earth itself." Sadly this was a classic piece of political humbug; for only two days previously the UK had blocked a proposal at a conference in the Netherlands for a 20 percent reduction in carbon dioxide emissions by 2005. By the time that year dawned global warming had become a mainstream issue. Sir Nicholas Stern, an internationally renowned economist, was commissioned to write a report on climate change. The report was published in 2006 and it is worth summarizing its simple and apocalyptic message. Climate change, says Stern, is fundamentally altering the planet. The simple scientific conclusion is that human activity has raised the amount of carbon dioxide in the atmosphere from 280 parts per million before the industrial revolution to its present level of 430. Trapping heat the gas has caused the earth to warm by more than half a degree, with a further half degree at least to come over the next few decades. If this continues the level will reach 550 parts per million by 2050 with the result that global average temperatures would be two degrees centigrade above pre-industrial levels and by the end of the century they would have risen by five degrees. Significant warming will profoundly change our planet, affecting the water cycle and so crop yields and producing disastrous effects on the oceans because of increasing acidity. "The impacts of climate change," says Stern, "are not evenly distributed. The poorest countries and people will suffer earliest and most." He refers to a World Health Organization estimate that climate change had killed 150,000 people since the 1970s, mainly in Africa. "Just one centigrade increase in global temperature above pre-industrial levels could double annual deaths from climate change to at least 300,000." As a footnote to this summary of the *Stern Report* we can note the fourth assessment report of the Intergovernmental Panel on Climate Change. Launching the report a senior UN official said that so strong is the evidence linking the warming climate to human actions that ignoring or denying global warming and its causes was the height of irresponsibility. In the face of apparently undeniable fact such irresponsibility has unfortunately been too obvious. The twentieth century did indeed see the rise and significant growth of the Green Movement; but it will be readily agreed by historians that there was no general change of attitude as a result. The reason is perhaps that if the Green Movement were to succeed then society would need to show the "old-fashioned" virtues of self-denial and humility. Insistence on such as essential virtues is, however, an important part of theological ethics. The fundamental failure of which the developed countries were guilty was the pretence that there was no need for self-denial. That was a moral failure since self-denial is an integral part of even a utilitarian ethic let alone a Christian one. Austerity is the direct opposite of the consumerism characteristic of the unrestrained acquisition encouraged by the political policies such as those advocated by Mrs. Thatcher, whose moral legacy is the ego-centricity that had bedevilled British society in the closing years of the twentieth century and beyond. Equally unappealing to a consumerist culture was the virtue of humility since such a culture is based on a notion of entitlement encapsulated in the popular advertisement slogan, "Because you're worth it." This has been a subtle and disastrous transformation of the moral concepts of rights rendering them void of ethical significance.

Faced with such a growing crisis the attitude of theology has been somewhat ambiguous. A century ago Feuerbach characterized the attitude of the Christian as subjective and unconcerned with the world in which he lived. "Nature, the world, has no value, no interest for Christians. The Christian thinks only of himself and the salvation of his soul."[1] By retreating into this interiority it could be said that Christianity now fiddles while the Rome of nature burns. Indeed it has been argued that the blame for the very crisis must be laid on the shoulders of Christianity. An American mediaeval historian, Professor Lynn White, published an article in 1967 that has been much quoted, entitled, "The Historical Roots of Our Ecologic Crisis." Attacking the anthropocentrism of Christianity, particularly in the Western church, he condemns the Judaeo-Christian attitude towards nature as arrogant. Thus, while Byzantine illustrations of Genesis 1:28 show Adam and the animals in repose in the Garden of Eden Western ones show Adam threatening the animals and the animals huddled together against him. White's trenchant comments are worth quoting:

> Our science and technology have grown out of Christian attitudes towards man's relation to nature which are almost universally held not only by Christians and neo-Christians but also by those who fondly regard themselves as post-Christians. . . . We are superior to nature, contemptuous of it, willing to use it for our slightest whim. . . . Both our present science and our present technology are so tinctured with orthodox Christian arrogance towards nature that no solution for our ecologic crisis can be expected from them alone. Since the roots of our trouble are so largely religious, the remedy must also be essentially religious, whether we call it that or not.[2]

1. Feuerbach, *The Essence of Christianity*, 287.
2. Appendix of Francis Schaeffer, *Pollution and the Death of Man*, 111, 114.

It is difficult for us to absolve the Christian tradition of all responsibility for this rape of fair nature, though I shall want to point out that it is not a simple issue. Consider for a moment, then, whence we get the notion of nature as something inanimate and so dead, something therefore disposable by man according to his desires and whims. The saying that the Sabbath was made for man has been extended without qualification to nature so that we have tended to think that the very value of nature is a function of man's own existence. As Ivan Illich puts it, our social demand is like a stomach that has had the bottom knocked out of it and into this bottomless pit we have stuffed the raw material of nature. For decades we have accepted and endowed the consumerist attitudes I mentioned at the beginning of this chapter and we have been lacking in our condemnation of the quasi-theologies that elevate entrepreneurial attitudes into moral and spiritual ideals. Thus we think, as we've already said, that nature is some virtually limitless storehouse of resources intended for human use. Man has, we've assumed, the commission to control nature for the purpose of improving the material standards of living, so science and technology are neutral means for serving our ends and bringing nature further and further under our control. Insidiously, these attitudes spread into more general moral assumptions such as that what *can* be scientifically known and technologically done *should* be known and done. I myself remember being involved in a bitter if not fierce discussion with some biological experimenters when I criticized this assumption that was made in the explanation of possible ramifications or perhaps elaborations of the experiment. The reply that I was given was that there was no point in knowing that something could be known if it were not in fact given that technological application. We have taken for granted that the successful human is the achiever in society. As these assumptions become more and more generalized they result in the confusion of spiritual and material categories. Thus freedom is thought of as either only discoverable in abundance or indeed something that is synonymous with abundance.

I have given White's argument so full and indeed sympathetic a hearing because it echoed so general an attitude in Christian society. Even now one can find a serious and not simply a populist reaction to any concern with an ecological crisis maintaining that Christians are too ready to accept prophecies of doom. Bjørn Lomberg has argued in his *The Skeptical Environmentalist* that creation is not in a state of collapse. If we distinguish environmental fact from myth, he says, a wide range of indications suggests that the world is becoming a better place in which to live. People are living longer, healthier lives and generally the context of life is not only good but showing every sign of becoming better. In developed countries pollution is decreasing and as poorer countries become richer they will pollute less. For Lomberg the calculation of costs and benefits is guaranteed to ensure the world's progress and not simply its survival. Regrettably this seems more like a classic piece of psychological denial than a reasoned response to the scientific predictions based on fact. It reminds one of the haunting paragraph in James Diamond's *How Societies Choose to Fail or Survive* in which he quotes research into the levels of fear among residents living in a narrow valley just below a dam. The closer the residents were to the dam the greater the fear of a dam burst; but then it stopped and those living within just a few miles of the dam indicated no fear.

To return to White, the condemnation was soon rejected as a one-sided argument, Francis Schaeffer's *Pollution and the Death of Man* (1970) being in part a response. By 1996 Michael Northcott could refer to a "flowering of ecotheology," which he traces.[3] To repeat the story would be tedious but it is interesting to look again briefly at the argument. If we begin with history, the evidence afforded by Keith Thomas in his book *Man and the Natural World: Changing Attitudes in England* 1500–1800 is that the Christian tradition has in fact also been extremely sensitive in its attitude to nature. Turning to the essentially theological issue we can think of the long and powerful tradition of Christian Platonism as having provided a very clear and moving picture of God *in* creation long before this emphasis was seen in the work of Moltmann. Again, the work of biblical exegetes should have left no one in any doubt that domination of nature has no place in the picture of the world offered in either the Old or the New Testament. From the opening pages of Genesis to the closing pages of Revelation the picture we are given is one of covenant and authority *under* God. I will neither weary my learned biblical colleagues with examples nor pretend to their erudition; but all of us recall now and again, whether the context is in cosmogony, poetry, or law, the *sole absolute* authority of God is emphasized in the Old Testament and man's place in the universe is interpreted in terms of covenant. As for the New Testament, there is no hint of domination in the Gospels; and St. Paul in the references he

3. Northcott, *The Environment and Christian Ethics*, 124–63.

makes to nature is concerned simply to develop our appreciation of the world as a creation along with man. What is more, in those references to what will be finally revealed he makes clear the inter-relation of man and nature. Perhaps the most remarkable and clearest counter-example to White's would be the talk in Revelation of a new heaven and a new earth. Space would not allow me even if I were competent to pursue the question through the history of Christian thought; but I am confident that it is not found even in the bold Shakespearean expressions of the philosophy of Renaissance. "I am master of my fate; I am the captain of my soul" is William Ernest Henley not Shakespeare. So I would want to point out that it is all too easy for theologians to fall into the trap of *indiscriminate* self-accusation. Beating our breast and wailing are no substitutes for the development of a proper approach to the question such as Moltmann sought in his Gifford Lectures.[4]

It may be worth pausing a moment before proceeding with this theological argument to recall some remarks Gorbachev made in his epoch-marking speech to the United Nations on December 7th, 1989. When I think of Gorbachev I cannot fail to be reminded of Isaiah's characterization of Cyrus as the Lord's "anointed." That is why I refer to the speech as epoch-marking rather than epoch-making. This is what he said:

> International economic security is inconceivable unless related not only to disarmament but also to the elimination of the threat to the world's environment. In a number of regions, the state of the environment is simply frightening. Let us . . . think about setting up within the framework of the United Nations a centre for emergency environmental assistance. Its function would be promptly to send international groups of experts to areas with badly deteriorating environments.

Now that the world has itself become a world issue we are thus witnessing a sea-change of political attitudes into something rich and strange, the solidarity of man faced with the awesome results of his own sin. Gorbachev's speech was an epoch-*marking* one—he was at once the expression of the problems and the advocate of a new way of looking for solutions. In this way he may well have been the modern Cyrus, an unconscious agent of the friendly work of a Providence who is never distant from the sighs and groans of creation. Let me begin my exposition of a theological answer by saying what it should not be. It seems to me

---

4. Moltmann, *God in Creation*, 22.

that the kind of theology that has been popular in modern Protestantism leads to a dead end as far as the ecological problem or crisis is concerned. The division of man into inner and outer has been developed to the detriment of any holistic theology of nature. For the theology of demythologizing and the reinterpretation of a worldview in terms of existentialist attitude of hope there is no ecological eschaton, no last days of nature. We hear a lot about the history of God with man but it seems to me a very peculiar history—far removed from the concrete history of man in his world which takes him far back to a beginning beyond his own history. This is why I find Bultmann very much a theologian of yesterday and I feel that today's theologian must be a more earthy character like Teilhard. "Where are the roots of our being?" asks Teilhard de Chardin in a particularly eloquent passage and he answers it thus:

> In the first place they plunge back and down into the unfathomable past. How great is the mystery of the first cells which were one day animated by the breath of our souls! How impossible to decipher the welding of successive influences in which we are forever incorporated!—however autonomous our soul, it is indebted to an inheritance worked upon from all sides—before ever it came into being—by the totality of the energies of the earth.[5]

It is worth hearing such an eloquent expression of modern man's appreciation of his links with nature because seldom does it get put in a theological idiom. As I say, the kind of theology that has been popular with us has left man alone and afraid as Housman described him. Even when such theology does not exclude the material world from its hope for the future it seems to me to be just as planned in its view of the temporal dimension. I often told students that I may be too simple-minded to understand the peculiar doctrine of a Pannenberg who tells us that the future has already occurred and that is what causes the present. But if I am then I say in all modesty so much worse for that theology. To attenuate the eschatology of the Bible so that it means simply some openness towards an empty future is to deny the very life-spring of Christian action. All the hope for a new world is left to perish with ancient mythology. With this kind of future which the threatened world of today expects with dread this kind of faith has nothing to do. Faith is open to a future which in the end is nothing but faith itself.

5. De Chardin, *Le Milieu Divin*, 30.

I count it my good fortune that the only person to teach me systematic theology was Paul Tillich because his theological thinking was done in cosmic categories. As he developed his theology in the 1920s he emphasized the impossibility of separating man from his world and as he ended his systematic exposition in the 1960s he saw the whole business of theology as linked with the single over-all work of life-creation. There have been too many occasions on which I have complained of a lack of clarity in Tillich so that when I say that as I read the theology of Moltmann I yearn for Tillich's clarity of outlook then I need say no more. Yet I must admit that Moltmann's theology is very clearly born of and addressed to the agonies of the second half of the twentieth century and as such demands our serious attention. It also demonstrates how various the theological motivations are to an ecological concern. The very titles of his books—*Theology of Hope*, *The Crucified God*, and *God in Creation*—show how his theology catches the moods and concerns of a dying century. The importance of this is that his theology is not characterized by some hermetically sealed religious concern but views religion as bound up with life in the world and creation as involved in the suffering of Christ and our future hope in Christ.[6] By taking seriously all the motifs of incarnational theology—the cross, being crucified with Christ, and being raised again in Christ—he stresses solidarity with suffering as part of a clear hope that is itself a dynamic of action.[7] The solidarity of Christ's suffering with ours had already been emphasized in *The Crucified God*. One of his great achievements in theology has been his determined effort to understand the Trinity from the basis of creation and history as distinct from the emphasis on God's transcendent relations. God as Father, Son, and Spirit is to be understood, he argues, in terms of cosmic activity. It could perhaps be said that this, as much as any Eastern Orthodox influence, is what has led him to stress the necessity of understanding God as a social Trinity. We have, he says, tended to see God as essentially the powerful monarch whose rule means the utter obedience of ourselves as his subjects (a view perhaps that one naturally carries away from Calvin's *Institutes* with its massive emphasis on God's *majestas*). The result of this is that we conceive our relation to the natural world in the same way, with the "dominion" spoken of Psalm 8 being understood as a domination. Such a view of God, he says, neglects the Trinitarian relationship, which

---

6. Moltmann, *Theology of Hope*, 136ff.

7. Moltmann, Cf. *Future of Creation*, 98–124.

is the reality of the divine being and consequently the proper basis for our understanding of ourselves and the world.[8] By this emphasis on the role of the Spirit in creation and his huge emphasis on the *kenosis* revealed in the cross Moltmann has made a unique contribution to our understanding of the continuing creative work of the Trinity.

The participation of creation in the glory of God is something Moltmann holds out as our hope. We can understand it by returning to the Genesis story of creation, which concludes with the Sabbath, the day when God rested from his labor to enjoy his creation, which he saw was very good. This is what we can anticipate when after our striving we rest in God.[9] It is interesting to compare this emphasis in Moltmann's work with the Pauline idea of creation groaning in travail awaiting its freedom (Rom 8:20–22). Just as Paul was rejecting the Stoic idea of a final conflagration so Moltmann rejects the pessimism of those who prophesy the doom that will be the inevitable consequence of our ecological prodigality. Some very clear lessons can be learned from Moltmann's argument in *God in Creation* and I want now to indicate some of them. In the first place we are made to appreciate how the doctrine of creation is at the very heart of theology not only as some kind of basic assertion but as a doctrine related to so many if not indeed all doctrines. This is why I very much approve of Moltmann's emphasis on its Trinitarian nature—the Father creates through the Son in the Holy Spirit. If we realize that this is creation—not some distant initiation of a mechanical action by some absentee singular god—then there is less likelihood of our ignoring the divine involvement in the world. Think only of this: if the Father creates through the Son then those creative functions of the carpenter at his bench in Nazareth are part of what we mean by both "God" and "the world." What we sing in the liturgy about the divine humility is at once the humility of God's creative act and the glory of his creation. It is the same kind of cosmic, if you like, this-worldly, thinking that attracts me too in Moltmann's talk about the "new kind of thinking about God" that for him is demanded by an ecological doctrine of creation, "The centre of this thinking . . . is the recognition of the presence of God *in* the world and the presence of the world *in* God."[10] I am not happy with the way in which Moltmann talks here because I think it can destroy the very notion

8. Moltmann, *The Trinity and the Kingdom of God*, 139–44.

9. Moltmann, *God in Creation*, 250–55.

10. Ibid., 13f.

of divinity that grounds our thinking about the world. God is neither a part nor the whole of the universe. Yet when we think of creation it is quite wrong to imagine it as a relation between two things otherwise separate. The world's existence is part of the mystery of God because without God's existence, his power of being or what the medievals called his self-caused existence or his aseity, nothing exists. That is the simple but powerfully philosophical assertion of the Fourth Gospel. Finally, I think it is very necessary for us to follow Moltmann in his connecting of creation with the motifs of the Messiah and the doctrine of redemption. It speaks of a future for which creation was made and in which it will be perfected.

Creation is "aligned towards its redemption."[11] So, despite the fact that much of this theological argument is, to my mind, dubious and mistaken I too want to have a doctrine of creation that gives me hope for the world on which I stand and of which I am a part. Man's creatureliness means that as against God his status is in the end only the same kind of status as the world. Furthermore, that creatureliness is the peculiar power of man. C. F. von Weizsacker, the German physicist, says that the future of man hinges on the question of power and he goes on to speak of this power in man, the image of God. To the question "What does that mean?" he answers "In non-mythical terms: the image in which God appears to man does not show what man is but what he might be."[12] What I am contending is that the doctrines of creation and redemption should make us missionaries of the earth. It is not for nothing that the Bible begins with the story of a garden; for the essence of a garden is not its productivity or its growth but its balance of all the features of biological life to form something that is beautiful. My main reason for working my garden is that I enjoy it—in the same way "God saw that it was good."

In his *Reflections on the Revolution in France* Burke said that society is a partnership between those who are living, those who are dead, and those who are unborn. It is a very moot point whether and in what sense we have *duties* to those who are unborn. Yet there is a very clear sense in which one of the pressing problems about the possibility of global death is the very real possibility of complete destruction which lies in the nuclear threat. We do not even need to contemplate nuclear war; for ours and every generation after Chernobyl will know the awful risks we take in

11. Ibid., 5.

12. Von Weizsacker, *The History of Nature*, 181.

the production of nuclear power. Some little time ago there was the likelihood that an East Midlands village was to be used for dumping nuclear waste and the prospect galvanized a whole community into protest. It was not only their own convenience or interest they considered—they were disturbed by the prospect of a terrible future and were unwilling to take this risk with the generation to come. Here again there are the same issues as we have seen in our earlier discussion and therefore there is the same need for the theologian to display the relevance of theological illumination. Yet when we reflect that not even the most dreadful accident or unforeseen disastrous consequence of our actions can match in horror the sheer devastation that is possible in nuclear war I need hardly say that a consideration of that issue is inescapable. In any discussion of global life and death the unthinkable scenario of a total destruction of countries, continents, or even the world is something that demands our scrutiny.

In the debate on the morality of nuclear arms as in the political discussion much has been made of the fact that they represent the only way to serve peace because they are the "great deterrent." So it is worth our while to begin with this argument and ask ourselves how good an ethical justification this is. The model that this adopts for understanding international relations is that of a society where the inability of each member to escape the consequences of a trust in their own exercise of force means that they are forced to accept conventional restraints of social justice. What is a deterrent? It has often been argued and sometimes still is that the death sentence is the ultimate deterrent and it is worth noting then that in such context we do see the relevance of talking of ultimacy. But what is meant is clearly that the fear of consequences will hold a man back from violent crime. Fear is something a man experiences and the deterrent then is the experience of imagining that something will happen to him. This is where the talk about the deterrent nature of nuclear arms is in one way very different. For the point that is insisted on again and again in discussions is that the Bomb will deter precisely because it will never be used. Thus it will be argued that while nuclear war as such might be immoral the *threat* of using the nuclear deterrent is not in itself immoral. This casuistry needs careful analysis. The idea of the Bomb's existence being a dissuasive from its employment is indeed what makes the argument intelligible as the contention that this is the way of establishing peace; but it is not clear that this dissuasive has any meaning other than the Bomb's possible use. Moreover if it were in fact used then clearly it is no longer a deterrent. But what seems to me so difficult to understand is how one can ever define the state of affairs that is thus feared. It might be argued that this is the whole problem of testing—empirical quantification of the theoretical calculations of force and consequent destruction that an armaments science devises. But what kind of a world is that? It is all very well to talk of balance, but anyone like myself who still has horribly vivid memories of walking the bar and all the other stupid exercises in Physical Education lessons will tell you that the constant adjustment of balance is a harrowing experience. Consider it well: if as a world we are committing ourselves to this constant search for a quantity of force that is somehow enough to stop the other, which cannot be strictly quantified, then is this not to make the whole system of international relations radically unstable?

For the moment I am not talking of force as such but simply of the "great deterrent." I cannot emphasize enough that the inherent danger of such a system is that we forget what in fact it was for; and instead of providing the context for the resolution of world problems it becomes a means of producing problems. For some years Westerners have been regaled with domestic analogies of the problems that face us as nation states and we have been urged to view the economy as some extended domestic larder, with the problems of striking, for instance, overcome by laying in more tins of canned food. If that is indeed the way to look at things political why is it that we are so blind to the ruthless selfishness that makes a bully run away with the prize when we engage in a domestic contest of conkers, marbles, or what have you? My point is that there is absolutely nothing in the notion of balance that rules out as impossible the refusal by one of the parties to exploit the very context and misuse it. From the Garden of Eden onwards our story has always been this misuse of what is not in fact ours. If what I have been arguing seems to anyone far-fetched or sentimental let them only reflect on all the discussion of tactical nuclear weapons, which are somehow thought to be morally more acceptable than the "great deterrent." That discussion is interesting and important if only because it *both* accepts that this is opening the door to something horrible *and* also rejects the very possibility of that occurring. Here once more I fail to see the sense of talking of an X that makes Y impossible—when you say that X will not in fact occur. Years ago I remember arguing this only to be told by a fellow-churchman that I was in fact deflecting the light of moral condemnation. I was distracting people's attention from those moral issues that are properly their concern to issues where their voice could not be heard. This is nothing less than hypocrisy doing the Freudian thing of blaming someone else for one's own faults in relation to them. It comes to mind once more when we witness in Britain a strange, insidiously jingoistic advance towards totalitarianism that then has the gall to preach to other countries about the necessity of democratic freedom. In the end, as the Negro spiritual would remind us, it is a case of *not* my brother *nor* my neighbor but *me* standing in the need of prayer.

To end on a properly general note let me find my way back from this personal confession to one of a common interest. In my remarks about personal responsibility I have tried to remember what has been taught us by prophet-theologians such as Bonhoeffer. We need to ask what it means to be a Christian today. That puts upon Welshmen such as myself the burden of recognizing the difference between 1904 (the year of the Welsh Revival) and 2007.[13] As one whose career was amidst the alien corn it is a difference of which I was poignantly aware. Gone is the situation of my childhood and youth and gone too are the political concerns. Yet I cannot forget that the word that was the challenge in 1904 remains for me the self-same challenge. Though professionally not a biblical scholar I must confess to being appalled by the slovenly and cavalier use of the Bible by those who are so ready to talk of nuclear war as if it were something that need not worry us. If I am right in arguing for this personal challenge it is because the Christ of the New Testament is the same yesterday and today. So Christianity is a matter of what is relevant here and now and it is at all times a message of the victory of powerlessness. Tillich speaks carefully and wisely of the problems of pacifism in his book *Love, Power and Justice*; but the thesis of the book is that ultimately the three are one. Now if that is so we cannot indulge in the pretence that there is some violence that is not subject to moral evaluation. If we fail to say that there is in such a scenario as nuclear war a use of power and show of violence that is simply illegitimate then we have sold the pass in any attempt to define modern politics in moral terms. Let me return to the argument of my teacher Tillich. If love, power, and justice have a unity in the nature of the power that grounds our universe then it is incumbent on the Christian theologian to recall us to a contemplation of him who in love died for us. I am not talking of some sentimental moving away from the world to the calm of the cloister but of the prophetic engagement that can say "I

13. This paper was given in 2007.

sat where they sat." It means—once more let me say it—recognizing that providence is not limited in His choice of a Cyrus. And when from such unlikely quotations one hears the condemnation of nuclear armament then to misquote Watcyn Wyn shall we be sinfully dumb?

I have discussed two very different problems as the possibility of global death and I have sought to end on a uniting positive note. In the earlier part of the discussion mention was made of hope and I want to conclude by making that assertion more specific. What I mean is that the Christian doctrine of creation is concerned with nothing less than the totality of God's relation with his handiwork. Ian Ramsey used to say that the doctrine was one of God and his attributes and that always struck me as removing the doctrine from anything concerning this world of ours. That was my misunderstanding. What Ramsey sought to emphasize was that the doctrine was in no way a cosmological theory and that whatever was said as an empirical account of the world's origins said little about the heart of the doctrine. If I say that I believe in God the Creator I view the world, the universe, time, and history as having a transcendent dimension. To continue on my positive note of conclusion let us remind ourselves of the scriptural and patristic teaching of a transfigured cosmos. At the end of *Summa Contra Gentiles* Thomas Aquinas says that since man will be clothed with glory so in its own way will the creation.[14] Amidst all the stern warnings and condemnations that a Christian theology brings to the world at the beginning of the twenty-first century there is, too, the positive message of hope—all things will be made new.

14. Aquinas, *Summa Contra Gentiles*, IV, 97.

Bibliography

Alvarez, A. *The Art of Sylvia Plath*. Edited by Charles Newman. Bloomington, IN: Indiana University Press, 1970.

Anselm. *Anselm of Canterbury*. 4 vols. Edited by Jasper Hopkins and Herbert Richards. New York: Mellen, 1974–75.

Aquinas, Thomas. *De Potentia Dei (On the Power of God)*. 3 vols. London: Burns, Oates, 1932–34.

———. *Scriptum super libros Sententianum*. 5 vols. Edited by M. F. Moos and P. Mandonnet. Paris: Lethielleux, 1929–56.

———. *Summa Contra Gentiles (On the Truth of the Catholic Faith)*. 5 vols. New York: Doubleday, 1955–57.

———. *Summa Theologiae*. Vol 9. Translated by Kenelm Foster. London: Eyre and Spottiswoode, 1963–.

Aries, Philip. *L'homme devant la mort*. Paris: Seuil, 1977.

Aristotle. *The Complete Works of Aristotle*. Edited by J. Barnes. Princeton: Princeton University Press, 1992.

Barr, James. *The Garden of Eden and the Hope of Immortality*. London: SCM, 1992.

Barth, Karl. *Dogmatics in Outline*. London: SCM, 1958.

Benjamin, Walter. *Illuminations*. Edited by H. Arendt, London: Cape, 1970.

Bowen, Euros. "Creigle." In *Elfennau*, 63. Llandysul, UK: Gwasg Gomer, 1972.

Brierley *et al*. "Neocortical Death after Cardiac Arrest." *The Lancet,* September 11, 1971, 560–65.

Catholic Bishops' Conference of England and Wales. *Abortion and the Right to Life: A Joint Statement of the Catholic Archbishops of Great Britain*. 1980.

Collingwood, R. G. *An Autobiography*. Harmondsworth, UK: Pelican, 1944.

Cullman, Oscar. *Christ and Time*. London: SCM, 1962.

de Pater, W. A. *Immortality: Its History in the West*. Leuven: Acco, 1984.

Dodd, C .H. *The Fourth Gospel*. Cambridge: Cambridge University Press, 1953.

Ebeling, Gerhard. *Word and Faith*. London: Fortress, 1963.

Eliot, T. S. *The Complete Poems and Plays*. New York: Harcourt, Brace & Co., 1952.

Enchiridion Symbolorum: A Compendium of Creeds, Definitions and Declarations of the Catholic Church. Edited by Peter Hunermann. San Francisco: Ignatius, 1991.

Fenn, Richard K. *The Persistence of Purgatory*. Cambridge: Cambridge University Press, 1995.

Feuerbach, Ludwig. *The Essence of Christianity*. New York: Harper and Row, 1970.

Fletcher, Joseph. "Ethical Aspects of Genetic Controls." *New England Journal of Medicine* 285 (1971) 776–83.

Frankl, Victor. *Man's Search for Meaning*. London: Random House, 1959.

Garaudy, Roger. *The Alternative Future*. Harmondsworth, UK: Penguin, 1976.

Greene, Marjorie. *The Knower and the Known*. London: Faber and Faber, 1961.

Gregory of Nyssa. *Adversus Macedonianos*. Library of Nicene and Post-Nicene Fathers, Vol. V. Translated by Philip Schaff and Henry Wace. Oxford: Christian Literature, 1893.

Hare, R. M. *Essays in Bioethics*. Oxford: Clarendon, 1993.

———. *Language of Morals*. Oxford: Oxford University Press, 1952.

Häring, Bernard. *Medical Ethics*. South Bend, IN: Fides, 1973.

Hart, H. L. A. "The Ascription of Responsibility and Right." In *The Proceedings of the Aristotelian Society*, 49 (1948–49) 171–94.

Heidegger, Martin. *Being and Time*. Translated by John Macquarrie and Edward Robertson. Oxford: Blackwell, 1967.

Herbert, George. *The Works of George Herbert*. London: Warne, 1878.

Hodge, A. A. *Outlines of Theology*. 1879. Reprint. London: Banner of Truth Trust, 1972.

Hoffman, Frederick. *The Mortal No: Death and the Modern Imagination*. Princeton: Princeton University Press, 1972.

Hughes, Ted. "Notes on the Chronological Order of Sylvia Plath's Poems." In *The Art of Sylvia Plath*, edited by Charles Newman, 187–95. Bloomington IN: Indiana University Press, 1970.

Jaspers, Karl. *Philosophie*. Berlin: Springer, 1932.

———. *Philosophy*. 3 vols. Translated by E. B. Ashton. Chicago: Chicago University Press, 1967.

Kierkegaard, Søren. *Concluding Unscientific Postscript*. Translated by David F. Swenson. London: Oxford University Press, 1945.

———. *Either-Or*. 2 vols. Kierkegaard's Writings, 2. Edited and translated by Howard V. Hong and Edna H. Hong. Princeton: Princeton University Press, 1988.

———. *Søren Kierkegard's Journals and Papers*. Translated and edited by Howard V. Hong and Edna H. Hong. Bloomington, IN: Indiana University Press, 1967.

———. *Søren Kierkegaards Papirer*. 20 vols. Edited by P. A. Heiberg and V. Kuhr. Copenhagen: Gyldendal, 1909–48.

Kleinig, John. *Valuing Life*. Princeton: Princeton University Press, 1991.

Levinas, E. *Ethics and Infinity*. Pittsburgh: Dubuque University Press, 1985.

Litton, E. A. *Introduction to Theology*. London: Clarke, 1960.

Locke, John. *The Reasonableness of Christianity*. Edited by I. T. Ramsey London: Black, 1958.

Lucas, J. R. *Responsibility*. Oxford: Clarendon, 1993.

Luther, Martin. *D. Martin Luther's Werke: Kritische Gesamtausgabe*. 127 vols. Köln: Bölaus Nachfolger Weimar GmbH, 1883–2009.

———. *Table Talk*. Translated by W. Hazlitt. London: Bell, 1895.

Mabbot, J. D. "Moral Rules." In *Readings in Contemporary Ethical Theory*, edited by Kenneth Pahel and Marvin Schiller, 206–24. London: Prentice-Hall, 1970.

———. "Punishment." *Mind* 58 (1939) 155–57.

Mace, C. A. "Hierarchical Organization." *The Sociological Review* 26 (October 1934) 373–92.

MacKinnon, D. M. *A Study in Ethical Theory*. London: Black, 1957.

Marenbon, John. *From the Circle of Alcuin to the School of Auxerre*. Cambridge: Cambridge University Press, 1981.

McCormick, R. A., S.J., "Genetic Medicine: Notes on the Moral Literature." *Theological Studies* 33 (1972) 531–53.

Moltmann, Jürgen. *The Crucified God*. Translated by R. A. Wilson and John Bowden. London: SCM, 1974.

———. *The Future of Creation*. Translated by Margaret Kohl. London: SCM, 1979.

———. *God in Creation*. The Gifford Lectures. Translated by Margaret Kohl. London: SCM, 1985.

———. *Theology of Hope*. Translated by James W. Leitch. London: SCM, 1967.

———. *The Trinity and the Kingdom of God*. Translated by Margaret Kohl. London: SCM, 1980.

Morgan, Densil. "'Plentyn y Dyfodol?' Gyrfa Gythryblus Ben Bowen." In *Ysgrifau Beirniadol* XVIII, edited by Gerwyn Williams, 181–217. Denbigh, UK: Gwasg Gee, 2007.

Motion, Andrew. *Keats*. London: Faber and Faber, 1997.

Niebuhr, Richard. *The Responsible Self*. 1963. Reprint. San Francisco: Harper and Row, 1978.

Noonan, J. T. Jr. *Contraception: A History of Its Treatment by the Catholic Theologians and Canonists*. Oxford: Oxford University Press, 1965.

Northcott, Michael. *The Environment and Christian Ethics*. Cambridge: Cambridge University Press, 1966.

Parkes, Colin Murray. *Bereavement: Stories of Grief in Adult Life*. London: Tavistock, 1972, and his seminal work, *Love and Loss: the Roots of Grief and its Complications*. London: Routledge, 2006.

Patrides, C. A. *The Grand Design of God*. London: Routledge and Kegan Paul, 1972.

Plath, Sylvia. *Ariel*. New York: Harper Perennial, 1965.

Plato, *Phaedo*. Edited and translated by John Burnet. Oxford: Oxford University Press, 1911.

Popper, Karl. *The Poverty of Historicism*. London: Routledge and Kegan Paul, 1957.

Quine, W. V. *From a Logical Point of View*. Cambridge: Harvard University Press, 1953.

Rahner, Karl. *Foundations of Christian Faith*. London: Darton, Longman and Todd, 1987.

———. *On the Theology of Death*. London: SCM, 1972.

Ramaziani, John. *Poetry of Mourning*. Chicago: Chicago University Press, 1994.

Ramsey, Paul. *Fabricated Man*. New Haven: Yale University Press, 1970.

———. *The Patient as Person*. New Haven: Yale University Press, 1976.

Sartre, Jean Paul. *Being and Nothingness*. London: Methuen, 1958.

———. *L'être et le néant*. Paris: Gallimard, 1943.

Schaeffer, Francis. *Pollution and the Death of Man*. Wheaton, IL: Tyndale House, 1970.

Schweiker, William. *Responsibility and Christian Ethics*. Cambridge: Cambridge University Press, 1995.

Taylor, A. E. *Faith of a Moralist*. 2 vols. London: Macmillan, 1930.

Teilhard de Chardin. *Le Milieu Divin*. London: Collins, 1960.

Tennant, F. R. *The Origin and Propagation of Sin*. Cambridge University Hulsean Lectures 1901/2. Cambridge: Cambridge University Press, 2012.

Thomas, Dylan. *Miscellany One*. Letchworth, UK: Dent, 1966.

———. *Miscellany Two*. Letchworth, UK: Dent, 1966.

————. *Under Milk Wood*. London: Dent, 1954.

Thomas, Gwyn. *Apocalups Yfory*. Cyhoeddiadau Barddas, 2005.

————. *Gwelaf Afon*. Denbigh, UK: Gwasg Gee, 1990.

Tillich, Paul. *The Courage to Be*. London: Collins, 1962.

————. *Systematic Theology*. 3 vols. Welwyn, UK: Nisbet, 1953–64.

Vandervelde, G. *Original Sin: Two Major Trends in Contemporary Roman Catholic Reinterpretation*. Lanham, MD: University Press of America, 1975.

Von Hugel, Baron F. *Essays and Addresses*. Vol. 2. London: Dent, 1933.

Von Weizsacker, C. F. *The History of Nature*. Chicago: University of Chicago Press, 1949.

Walter, Tony. *The Eclipse of Eternity: A Sociology of the Afterlife*. London: Macmillan, 1996.

Warnock, Mary. *Nature and Mortality* London: Continuum, 2003.

Weil, Raymond. "Aristotle's View of History." In *Articles on Aristotle, 2: Ethics and Politics*, edited by Jonathan Barnes, Malcolm Schofield, and Richard Sorabji, 202–17. London: Duckworth, 1977.

Werblowsky, Z. "On Studying Comparative Religion." *Religious Studies* 11 (1975) 145–56.

White, Lynn. 'The Historical Roots of our Ecologic Crisis'. An appendix to Francis Schaeffer's *Pollution and the Death of Man* (as above).

Williams, Bernard. *Problems of the Self*. Cambridge: Cambridge University Press, 1976.

Williams, Glanville. *Textbook on Criminal Law*. 1978. Reprint. Universal Law, 2003.

Williams, N. P. *The Idea of the Fall and Original Sin*. London: Longmans, Green & Co., 1927.

Williams, Raymond. *Border Country*. London: Hogarth, 1988.

Winch, Peter. *The Idea of a Social Science and Its Relation to Philosophy*. London: Routledge and Kegan Paul, 1958.

Wittgenstein, Ludwig. *Tractatus Logico-Philosophicus*. Translated by C. K. Ogden. London: Routledge, 1922.